To
Jane.

All part of the
incredible journey.

CW00739988

Cb
Andy
7-2-15.

HOW TO SEDUCE

YOUR WIFE

(or anyone else's)

Andy Gibney

How to seduce your wife (or anyone else's)

Text Copyright © Andy Gibney 2015

Andy Gibney has asserted his right in accordance with the Copyright Designs and Patents Act 1988 to be identified as the author of this work.

All rights reserved
No part of this publication may be lent, resold, hired out or reproduced in any form or by any means without prior written permission from the author and publisher. All rights reserved. Copyright © 3P Publishing

First published in 2015 in the UK by 3P Publishing

Set in Electra LT Regular

3P Publishing
Tailby House, Bath Road
Kettering, NN16 8NL

A catalogue number for this book is available from the British Library

ISBN 978-0-9731748-0-3

Cover design: Jamie Rae
www.jamierae.co.uk
Cover model: Kim Armstrong

Without those years of listening to her talk when my sister and I were very small, I would never have become such a good listener and collector of stories, so for that thank you, Diana Gibney, my mother. When you read this think back to those days in South London and how far we've travelled.

Contents:

Acknowledgements   1

Introduction – I'd better explain myself   5

Chapter 1 – How you seduced your wife   13

Chapter 2 – She's had enough   23

Chapter 3 – It began with Michael Caine   35

Chapter 4 – The journey begins   47

Chapter 5 – The grooming survey   69

Chapter 6 – The sex survey   79

Chapter 7 – Time to start understanding the issue   103

Chapter 8 – They want to be loved   125

Chapter 9 – And now we begin   153

Chapter 10 – Is it time to stray?   161

Chapter 11 – The softer touch   171

Chapter 12 – Shall we bring a friend?   185

Chapter 13 – What else could there be?   205

Chapter 14 – It's time to go   211

Chapter 15 – Sleeping with the enemy   225

Chapter 16 – The end is really the beginning   237

Bibliography   257

About the author   260

Acknowledgements

There is no creative endeavour as solitary as writing a book, except perhaps painting, and yet I still find myself profusely grateful to so many people for the creation of this particular title. This lends itself to the Oscar speech and of not wanting to leave anyone out. The challenge in this is that many of the participants have taken part under the cloak of anonymity and shall remain so and it this group that I first extend my thanks. The myriad of souls whose stories I have been told, the people who shared their sexual secrets (an even larger thank you to those whose stories did not get told due to space) and to those who passed on stories, experiences and research which has made this book such a fascinating journey.

From the beginning of this process Shanette Freeman supported me along the way. She has given me belief, helped with the frustration and believed in every word. A more staunch supporter would be difficult to find. We bounced, crashed, cruised and ran through the year it was being written.

Hayley Clare became an ever closer friend through a trying time and made me laugh, sometimes intentionally, she listened when things got difficult and her level of support has been truly beyond measure. An extended thank you to Robin Clare as well for his support, even when he was shaking his head in utter disbelief.

Becky Adams, an established author and media presence in her own right, has been a constant source of advice and is the only person whose name I have used without change, completely with her permission. Becky's tales will amuse and surprise you as you hear her opinions and tales of the dark side of Milton Keynes and the Home Counties. Her experience of publishing her own award winning book was shared so willingly in telephone conversations and in random meetings across Northamptonshire. I listened to every word Becky and most of it made a difference.

Joanne Pearson, to say all I owe her would be to give away some of the secrets contained herein, but what I can say is that without her I would probably have never have become a writer. Jo and I share a long past and we have remained friends throughout many twists and turns and I know she'll be wanting one of the first signed copies.

What of my draft copy readers? Denise Knowles, Rick Wills, Jamie Rae, Anita Noon and two of the guests stars mentioned already, Hayley Clare and Becky Adams. What a fantastic job you did, helping me turn a pile of paper into a living book. Yes, books live, of course they do!

Robin Sharpe sat and listened to me as I explained my hopes and dreams for 'Seduce' and shared my enthusiasm for the future. His living room became our dream factory, only time will tell if those dreams are achieved. Daniela Gugliuzza never doubted I'd finish this book and encouraged me along the way, even when I disappeared off the radar for weeks at a time. When I first showed Nigel Botterill the cover his face exploded in delight and he said I was on a winner. Affirmations like that made so much of a difference, us creative types can be so fragile and his conviction strengthened my back bone.

The terrific team at Marvellous PR – Lucy Matthews, Lisa Balliache and Louise Barnett are out there telling the world about me and this book even when the world was out there saying "Who?" "What?" Like the three musketeers I am their d'Artagnan.

In April 2014 a chance meeting in an art gallery brought me into contact with Kerry Ambler. She is a poet of some note in the Northamptonshire region, she has a heart of gold and I remember sitting at her kitchen table when I first told her the book title. She laughed as she often does and has since called me 'Andy the Writer'. I love this description, although only you, as a reader, will determine if her assessment was correct. Kerry introduced me to the world of poetry, spoken word and performing in the area where I live. It was here that I met Justin Thyme, Peter James Norman, Jimtom James and, in turn, Kenneth Nash and Robert James Reeves. Throughout 2014 I stood on stages reading parts of the book, blogs and anything that came into my head to audiences which ranged from polite to downright enthusiastic. All of this built my confidence in the book and the message I was trying to convey. Without Kerry none of that would have happened so my level of gratitude to her is enormous. Her advice about reading the book aloud was one of the best pieces I heard all year.

It was through Kerry that I met Nathan Jones. Although we are so different we share our love of words and have become confidantes and friends, he has given me exactly what I need, when I needed it and what I needed was honesty. If I wrote something, shared it with him and he didn't like it he told me so and he told me why. As a writer this has been invaluable.

The cover design was done by Jamie Rae, with an original idea from his partner in crime, Craig Hayward. We worked on it and brought it closer and closer until it has become what it is now. As well as the cover, Jamie has worked with me on video and photography for years and it's great that I can give him the thanks he deserves in these pages. Kim Armstrong is the cover model and a fantastic job she has done too, with additional help on that shoot from the lovely Stacy Coles.

All of the print process was covered by Janice Pretot at *Eazyprint,* My thanks go to the team there, especially Jordan Rzymski, for his tweaks in the final design.

As this process drew to its conclusion, Noah Donnelly appeared almost ghost-like to take charge of the final edit, correcting all of my considerable grammar mistakes and we worked together late into the night and early into the morning tightening this script, this sheaf of papers and thoughts. All credit goes to him to for making the book flow in the most efficient way.

Which finally brings me to Caroline Snelling. There have been a few people who believed in this project from the beginning, but hardly any as much as Caroline. The fact that you are reading these words is because she supported me in a way that no-one else did. The last few months of bringing the book to print were bumpy, filled with trepidation and not without fear. Caroline helped me ride the waves, with a hand on the tiller to guide the book from stormy ocean to calm harbour. My thanks are beyond measure.

Introduction

I'd better explain myself

How do I grab you from the first line, the first sentence, the first page? How do I keep you throughout this tome, this insight into love in the 21st Century? I must seduce you, I must keep you engaged, interested and intrigued. For a book of this size that could be a challenge so I'll outline some of what lies ahead. It took a year to write, with the first draft, others' contributions, compiling of data and bringing it to its final state of completion. There were times when I left it alone and times when it consumed my every waking hour. It could be said that writing this book was like a relationship itself.

Many of you will ponder the sex survey, every word is true and the people are real. Some of you will smile at the grooming survey, women can be so honest. You might find the six ways of trying to keep your relationship together either intriguing or extreme. Some of the attitudes expressed might annoy you, some might challenge the way you think and sometimes they might make you smile.

My job, as the writer, is to keep you with me until the end for it is the end that holds the greatest secrets. You will be tempted to turn there now, but you won't have to because I have begun the book with part of the end (in the first chapter). If you have seen 'American Beauty' you will remember that Kevin Spacey narrates the film from the end and I have taken this approach as well. In order to know where you are going you must first know the destination. The journey may be full of twists and turns, but the destination must be kept in sight.

The book started as a guide for men, but as the process went along I became more convinced that it would have more female readers than male. I think it is possible that they will read it first and then they will tell their husband/boyfriend/partner to read it. Some men will ignore them and tell their wife/girlfriend/partner that they can't be taught anything from a book. They will be the men who find themselves being cuckolded by someone else. Do you know why? Because most men believe they already know what a woman wants and many women expect him to know what she wants. He thinks it's a man to do the DIY, to earn the money, to cut the grass and to be their knight in shining armour. There are elements of truth in this, but women want so much more and most men never look beneath the surface. This book examines every facet of love from the initial attraction, to the first throes of love to the waning and how to keep it fresh and exciting. It will also cover those women being controlled and it will help you find the answers if you have to leave. Literally from conception to death, but in a relationship way.

It will take you on a journey; one that many of you won't have been on before. You will be taken into the mind of the player, those sexual predators on both sides of the sexes; it will take you into romance; you will come along on the journey of sexual psychology, sexual politics and why most stereotypes are embraced rather than rejected. This is not about Mars and Venus, far from it. (John Grey's seminal book on relationships published in 1992 which claimed that the sexes are from different planets, metaphorically, not actually). I will illustrate this tale with real life examples, but all the identities will be hidden. If you have known me then fear not from any revelations – a lady's secrets will remain so, but the tales will be told.

What does a man know about the way a woman thinks? Since 2002 I have been a therapist, at first curing people's life-long phobias and then seeing people for more and more psychological ailments. As the book trundles along I will explain how I learned the things that helped me understand human beings in a deeper way. Most of my clients have been women, I'm sure that's not a massive surprise (it's usually women who discuss their feelings), but what surprised me was how many of them came to talk to me about the problems they were having with their relationships.

Someone might come in with a very simple problem like not being able to sleep properly and then realise that she was no longer in love with her partner. Someone else would come in and sit, in floods of tears, wondering how she could escape the nightmare of a relationship she was in. The more people I spoke to the more I was amazed at how inept so many men were at keeping their partners happy. In the middle of this time scale I left my long term partner and went on something of a sexual awakening, experiencing dating in the internet age and realised two things. The first was that there is a greater availability of partners than ever before, but at the same time so much felt so shallow. If you've ever had dinner with your friends and they are on their phone checking up and talking to someone else you'll know exactly what I mean. In an age of the greatest connectivity of all time we are the most disconnected we've ever been.

I believe in love, I believe in romance, I also believe in amazing sex and a life full of cuddling and kissing. There will be some of you nodding your head now and others trying to work out what the hell I'm on about. Seduction equals sex doesn't it? That's the way a man's mind works – will she go down on me? Will she be like a porn star? What will she like? A woman is interested in emotion – how will she feel? Will he make her feel like a princess? That's not to say that women don't like sex, quite the contrary. They love it, but you, if you're a male, will only get her best when you make her want to give it to you; and most men fail miserably at this. If you're a woman, you will probably be agreeing. So, yes, I believe in love, and the fact is I have had affairs with married women and none of those women would have the slightest interest in me if the man they had at home knew how to make them feel desired. Make her feel like a princess and she will become your queen.

To explain the point – to have a woman fall in love with you your task is to stimulate her in many ways; she has to feel safe with you and you have to help her feel that no one else holds your interest other than her. Pretty much everyone understands this, but what happens as a relationship ages is that men (typically, but women do it too) forget to make the other person feel special. If you do that for long enough, no matter how much they loved you to start with, there will come a point when someone else shows an interest and then you are in trouble. A phrase to conjure with is "One person's rejection is another's erection." It's flippant, a little crude and completely true.

A more musical explanation of the same sentiment is in the song *Jimmy Mack* by Martha Reeves and the Vandellas :

> "Jimmy, Jimmy, oh Jimmy Mack, when are you coming back?
> My arms are missing you, my lips feel the same way too
> I tried so hard to be true, like I promised I'd do
> But this boy keeps coming around,
> He's trying to wear my resistance down"

Jimmy Mack knows what he is doing. Whatever her fella is doing it's not keeping his eye on Martha and Martha is pleading with him to get a grip, but men so often don't listen, don't observe and certainly don't feel or know when their lady is unhappy. I've done it myself. Ignored the signs and then wonder why I got dumped, I was in my 20's and it devastated me, but eventually the pain passed. Later on I was madly in love with a girl, we had a lot of ups and downs and eventually parted because we went in opposite directions. After we broke up for a little while I wasn't sure where my place was in the dating world. It had all changed in the years we had been together (as you might find out yourself) and then I discovered that women found me attractive. This was a total surprise to me. I had been with someone whom I thought was beautiful and I felt grateful that she was with me and then a much younger woman found me attractive and we went out together. When it finished I started to look at the big wide world. I talked to friends of mine who had been on dating sites and sought their advice. What I learned would change my life forever and maybe it will change yours as well.

If you have been in a relationship for a long time (more than ten years) then the world of dating has changed beyond recognition. Social media has seen to that. It has never been easier to cheat on someone, or to develop relationships, to stay in touch with a lover from afar or merely to make friends. Another trend has been people getting back together who were once sweethearts many years ago. Perhaps their partner died or has left them and they find that love is sweeter the second time around. Facebook, match.com, Twitter and any of those social networking sites changed the rules for relationships and you had better know about them, but far more importantly you had better know about yourself and your partner.

Love, as has been said by those wiser than me, makes the world go round. And yet it dies so readily, people allow life to become so ordinary so easily. Love is that magical unseen substance known only to two people for all other things stop and the world seems to revolve around them – they create their own world and their own bubble. You and I will explore why this magic stops, but we will also learn how to keep it alive; how to keep that person who means so much to us wrapped in our arms.

If you have come to this as a player perhaps you will learn that there is more to life than the thrill of the next conquest and that the empty feeling you have when you return home or they walk out the door can be transformed by the one who moves your soul.

I am a romantic. Not a Shelley or a Byron, but the one who finds beauty in a rock song like "Everlong" by the Foo Fighters with its gorgeous line "Breathe out so I can breathe you in." The one who finds it in the caress on the sofa on a Saturday night watching "The X Factor". I believe in love, I believe in romance and I believe in lust. It keeps me alive, it fills me with joy when I awake and it made me want to write this book.

I don't, for a minute, believe that all men are romantics, nor women either, but I am utterly convinced that we all want to be loved. I have only spoken about heterosexual relationships so far, but I also touch on the world of gay and lesbian relationships as well. The Beatles weren't joking when they said that "All We Need Is Love" and Marti Pellow and Wet, Wet, Wet also got it right when they interpreted Reg Presley's lyrics for "Love Is All Around".

Without it we crave it, with it we often feel like we have gone mad and often we have. Love will make you soar and it will bring you crashing to the ground. This book, based on 7 years of my own personal journey, in addition to 12 years as a therapist and to everyone who has contributed in written, or for want of a better phrase, oral form thank you, but also you, the reader, should thank these contributors for furthering our collective knowledge and moving us forward in the matter of human relationships. The most challenging of our daily interactions, but also the most rewarding. Research tells us time and again that people who live together, in a happy relationship, live longer, better lives.

As animals we are not designed to walk alone, although many of us crave time to be on our own, and when we are alone, on windy November nights with silence in the house and rain cascading off the windows we remember the times when arms held us tight, when lips crushed ours and we awoke to a smile, a cuddle and "good morning".

If you are in a relationship then it is my hope that this book makes you examine where you two are and where you are going. To stand still is to slip backwards and this book, about more than anything, is about the future.

Thank you for buying, stealing or borrowing this piece of literature and enjoy the journey, the rollercoaster, the winding road of love as experienced through the eyes of this author and may it bring you more joy, more knowledge and more application to find your place in the emotional world.

Andy Gibney
Weldon, 12th January 2015

Chapter 1

How you seduced your wife

For me, to be in love is about three distinct areas: physical, emotional and spiritual.

The physical is always the easiest to understand. If you are intensely attracted to someone then the emotions are affected anyway, obviously you get turned on, but you will also find your heart leap, your life feels better immediately and there is sunshine everywhere you look. A smile, a kiss, a gentle touch, all elicit emotions of passion and happiness, serotonin and oxytocin is released and you float off into the world of love. Can you have great sex without love? Yes, you can. Can you have love without great sex? I'd argue it's more difficult. I understand that you can be in love with someone and do a lot of things that don't involve sex, but great, passionate, heart stopping sex fuels your passion even further. To wrap someone up in your arms is to feel a closeness that you can't get from anywhere else. Most of my writing of the last few years has been fuelled by the passions that women have stirred up in me. My understanding of loneliness, my coping mechanisms, my desire to give every part of myself has been driven by someone whom I loved. It started with a kiss and it was driven by crazy, wonderful sex, but that wasn't all. The gentle touch of a hand in a darkened cinema, walking in the countryside and holding hands, just to look at the one you love sitting on a rock by a gurgling stream, all of this is the physical manifestations which have affected me so deeply at an emotional level.

The emotion of love is so all consuming it is true that you do actually go mad, that to think of that person who fills your heart with joy can stop all thoughts in your tracks. To feel love so deeply that you forget to breathe and only become aware of it when you have to take the next breath. To hold someone in your arms on a chill morning and smell their hair as they snuggle tighter into your chest. How can emotions not be intrinsically linked? And finally to the spiritual. That feeling beyond emotion, beyond the most intense orgasm, beyond even the thrill of looking at each other in the moment your eyes lock together, when you go beyond what you think is physically and emotionally possible and reach a high you have never reached before. To give yourself so deeply to someone that you are convinced they will never be interested in another person again. To give all of this and to be touched like a person catching the most beautiful sunset, the sound of your baby's first cry or your mother's "I love you", to feel all of this is to transcend all previous love. To know that no matter what, you must be with this person for the rest of your life, as long as the love flows and you keep being connected.

Do you remember the first time you saw her? Do you remember how you felt when you saw her? Did she make an immediate impression? Did you make an immediate impression on her? Or was it a case of not liking her at first and she grew on you? My parents were like that – or rather my step-father and mother were like that. My mum told me that she thought he was an arrogant bloke and she didn't like him at all. Something must have worked though, they've been together 43 years now.

I've fallen in love four times and I remember the first time I saw them all. The first was at work, the second was a new student starting a beginners class at my martial arts school, the third I opened the door and there she was and the last time was also a student who came to a class. All of them had the 'wow' factor, where inside you can hear yourself saying "wow" – and then trying to be cool and not let you make a fool of yourself. How long it took before I started dating them varied massively; the first was a few weeks, the second a few months, the third a couple of months and the last one was three and a half years. That is not to say that is how long it took to fall in love, that is how long it took to get a date. After that first date (which you should view very much as an audition) in every case things built up a head of steam very quickly indeed. In every case I was in love in under a month; the last time took about a week longer than the others as I was still dealing with all the barriers I had up by then. The single guy thing takes a while to get out of your head.

So, think back to your own experience – and this will work for the girls as well as the boys thinking about this process. How did you win the person you are with now or the great love of your life? Some of this will come up again when we look at how players seduce your wife or someone else's. The principal places that we meet our partners these days remain at work, on a night out or through a joint connection, but increasingly people are also meeting partners online. However it happens we all remember that first date. There are usually nerves involved, or at the very least a heightened level of anticipation. You dress to impress, however that may be. You shave (as a bloke – women shaving their facial hair is never going to be a selling point), you shower, you make an effort to smell nice, that your breath won't bowl over any dogs as you walk to the coffee shop/restaurant, wherever, you will also take time over your hair and do everything you can to make a good impression. Remember, the first date is the audition; this is not the goal. The goal is to find someone you want to spend more time with – whether that is a few hours or the rest of your life.

If you're smart you will have met in a coffee shop (again more on this in a later chapter) and now you are sitting there looking across from each other playing the sizing up game. You try not to be obvious – the men try not to look at her boobs (not always the easiest thing to do), we also look for signs that the girl is interested. Particularly difficult for men who struggle to understand subtle signs and body language, in fact sometimes a girl could actually wear a sign saying "Please kiss me" and they still wouldn't get it. The girl sits across from the guy reading his face, his posture, taking in his smell, his tonality and all the time she is searching for the incongruencies. There is a whole science dedicated to reading micro-expressions as well as the art of cold reading. What's cold reading? The method by which psychics appear to be psychic. I don't believe in psychic ability at all, but I do believe we can learn to tune in to other people. Human beings give away an awful lot of information in their body language, the tone in the way that they speak and their facial expressions. Cold reading is the method by which psychics learn things about you to appear to have foresight. Anyone can learn it; the simple fact is that most women are better than most men at reading people. Men, mostly deal in facts and data, whilst women react to emotion and communication. In the dating game this puts men at a massive advantage.

All of which brings us back to that first date. The awkwardness of the first moments (do you shake hands? Hug? Greet each other like Europeans with a kiss on each cheek), who buys the first drink? (I recommend the man always does this), the choosing of a table to sit at and the first parts of the conversation. Throughout that first hour (or two), although I had a friend who limited first meetings to fifteen minutes, you spend the whole time deciding if you want to spend more time with that person. The truth of it is, of course, that you have probably decided if you want to see each other again within the first minute of the meeting, such is the importance of first impressions. All of this I will deal with in much greater depth later, for now I want you to concentrate on the time when you and your partner had your first date and the emotions you were feeling at the time. If it's going well you will want it to continue won't you? We'll assume this is a going well date, but let me help you if it isn't.

A moment to digress. You realise – in the first two minutes – that this is not your dream date and you wish you hadn't taken the time to shave, shower and floss as it appears she has not done any of these things (or perhaps it's just incompatibility) – and before you think this is just about the guys, it's not, these same rules apply to the girls as well. First of all, always be polite. If it's an internet date we know that people don't always look like their photos. I've met ladies who look much nicer than their photos and ladies who don't – either way the rule is the same. Be polite; you've both gone there with expectations and there is always that chance that you don't look so great to them either. I know, amazing isn't it? I had one friend who turned up to meet a guy at a supermarket café – it's just coffee, that's fine. As they found a table the guy made an excuse to use the toilet (again really you should go before you get there but nerves can kick in), except that this peasant buggered off and left my friend sitting at the table. Outrageous behaviour and can really dent a persons' confidence. Remember in these circumstances that the other person is completely ignorant and you had a lucky escape.

In our scenario let's assume things are going well. You have been pleasantly surprised by how they look, they seem to like you too and the conversation is flowing. Even more so because you asked if she would like a super-sized bourbon biscuit and she accepted. You chat, you munch, you look at each other all the time and she is giving you the knee point and she's stroking her hair occasionally. Classic signs that she likes you. An hour passes. She asks if you would like another drink and you accept, offering to pay first of all, but you strike lucky and she says this one is on her. A good sign that she might have her own money and not be out to fleece you.

Another hour passes and you are getting on great. The signs are good. In fact so good you decide to move on somewhere else. That somewhere else may be your house, her house, a pub for lunch or dinner. Anywhere really, the point is you clearly like each other and all sorts of things are happening. Hormones are being released, serotonin is flowing around your body, dopamine is being created and you are in a very happy place. You can't wait to see this person again or more to the point you two want to find a place where you can rip each other's clothes off and see if the present is as good as the packaging. Glory hallelujah it is and you find yourself falling in love with the vision of beauty and so it has begun. The fairytale has been told and you two are Cinderella and her prince or in some cases Shrek and Princess Fiona. Life moves on a pace and you find yourself wanting to get married and as we have seen this may happen at any time from 17 to 87, although you'd have to think that 'Death us do part' has a higher chance of coming true at 87 rather than 17.

Love blossoms and flourishes, you decorate your house, you bring up children, you build a business and you build a life and somewhere along the line you stop going out to the movies or for dinner, the beautiful face no longer inspires you and you talk to the guys at work about how "she never stops moaning," or you repeat that oft told joke. "How do you get your girlfriend to stop giving you a blowjob?" "Marry her." And you think this is hilarious, no matter how many times you tell it.

The sex becomes ordinary, or you stop talking about it. You stop engaging on an emotional level and its either a five minute quickie so the kids can't hear you or maybe it's a regular Friday or Saturday night thing. Or worse still it stops altogether because you're tired or she's tired. The kissing which was once so passionate is now a peck in the morning before you leave for work and when you come home you slump in front of the tv too tired to even converse in intelligent or interesting conversation. The normal homecoming question "How was your day dear?" becomes a variation of the husband who was left for repeating "Same shit, different day." What you don't realise though is that not only is your love affair or marriage dying, but so are you. You have become your parents and your grandparents. You have become old and you don't have to be middle-aged for it to happen either. How many clients did I see whose husbands or wives were in their early thirties and when they came in you could have sworn they were ten years older? You forget that first date, that first kiss, that first night together. You forget it all and allow life to take over, accepting what everyone else thinks, in other words "Well that's what happens isn't it? You can't always live in fantasyland." And the person who accepts that is on the inexorable slide towards separation – it might take a few months or it could take years and if it does no one is getting out of that without feeling the pain.

As I explained in the introduction this book is about a couple of things. It is either you trying to keep your wife, or it is the wife who wants to teach the husband how to keep her, but others will also gain knowledge here. The single man who is looking for a partner will find rich pickings in the world of the bored wife (yes they really exist), but equally the bored wife will learn the tricks of the player and the insincere scoundrel. I hope it will broaden your horizons as well and that you will not judge too harshly those who find different avenues to explore.

One thing is for certain – all relationships are based on communication and if yours revolves around the kids, work, football or sport, and doesn't tap the wealth of human experience I guarantee one of you will have had enough. Never ever forget, "One person's rejection is another's erection." Don't take each other for granted, make the time to find the moments of love and keep working at it. If you love her or him, then make sure they know. No one gets bored of being told that you love them unless they have fallen out of love with you, then it is really bloody annoying, especially if they have fallen for someone else. What do you do if that happens? All the answers are coming in the following pages, even if you doubt me and don't think this 'method' will work. I promise you it does. If love was there once it can be found again, but to do it you have to know how to recreate those coffee shop moments and the magic that was once there.

I've tried to be wise and I have stood on the shoulders of giants: Allan and Barbara Pease, John Grey and Alfred Kinsey, but I have come at this subject (if you excuse the visual there) from a man living in a fast changing world. Where social media and the internet has made everything so much faster and how relationships can form and founder in a week and that to keep a love affair strong is, arguably, more difficult now than at any time in human history. As a man I have tried to get across the female perspective, whilst also trying to stay in touch with my male audience. If you were to think of the introduction and this chapter as the planning and getting the car ready then now it's time to start the ignition, put the car in gear and set off on the road.

Key points to remember:

1 **Physical, emotional and spiritual – each leading to the other and building on each other.**
2 **How it all began and how you fell in love.**

3 **Good manners.**

4 **How quickly things can go from amazing to ordinary.**

5 **Communication is key.**

Chapter 2
She's had enough

How do you know the signs are there? As a bloke, you're thinking "What signs?" There will be men reading this who won't have a clue that their wife is having an affair and have now looked over the top of this book to look at their wife and think "Beryl? No chance." However, if you're not keeping her happy there will be lots of men who would. At this point the more disbelieving will fall out of their chair laughing and be tempted to put this book down or aim it at the nearest waste paper basket. I mean, two things are going on here aren't they? One, who would have her and two, why would she leave you?

Again you are going to sit there and think "But I'm not rejecting her, I look after her (and the kids), I bring home food for the table and I make sure the car is clean and the grass is cut". What you are doing is thinking like a man and although many will doubt that you can really do this, if you want to keep her then you need to think more like a woman. The problem is that many men can't. They are locked into the way they think and nothing is going to change them, as we become older we become even more ingrained in the way we think and do things and to change is to cause pain, but pain for who? We all change as we get older, but often we narrow our view of the world rather than widen it.

Think of who you were at 15 or 20 years old. How have you changed since then? Even if you are only 5 years older how much have you changed? If you are now in your fifties then you would probably hardly recognise yourself and yet as we age through our relationships as individuals we change and yet as a couple we try to stay the same. It's like trying to keep a baby chick inside an egg, at some point it has to break out of the shell. There are two major causes of marriage or relationship splits, control or neglect.

If you feel that there is a problem in the relationship, and many times people ignore that nagging feeling that something isn't quite right, there are different ways that people try to make it right. One of those ways is spending money; that could be in terms of gifts, allowing your partner to use the credit card for shopping sprees, holidays or possibly cars. This is supposed to make the other person feel more for you. It can work at first, you are being made to feel wanted, but after a while you will start to feel 'bought'.

Another way is to force your affection on the other person, to keep telling them that you love them, trying to force them into mental submission to your will. Trying to make someone feel something doesn't work; if you 'win' will she feel like she's 'lost'? You can push people or you can pull them; I have found most consistently that people react better to being pulled – to allow them to think and develop. Again, many men don't understand this and try intimidation, either through aggression or through subtle mind control. This is often done so well that when it is pointed out to someone it takes them a while before they can see what is happening.

The opposite of this is neglect, often done completely unintentionally, but the couple drifts apart after time, where one person gets completely wrapped up in something that absorbs them. That can be work, a hobby, an interest or fascination. Many times as a therapist I had women telling me that their husband only talked about work or that he was too busy; that he would do just one more thing and then he would be there for her. Other stories were of him being completely absorbed in something that fascinated him: sport was popular, following a football team or going fishing. Or it could be that his friends were more important to him than she was: he 'had' to go out on a Friday night to see his mates, coming home after a skin full and then trying to 'seduce' her smelling of beer and maybe a curry.

At the time that this book is being written I have never known so many relationships coming to an end; it's just one of those things, or is it? I'm going to investigate some ideas from a few break ups. As a man you might recognise these traits in yourself or if you are a woman reading this you may question your own relationship. All names are changed for obvious reasons.

Jill had been married for 10 years; she married very young, mostly to get away from a father who tried to control her life and she wasn't about to be controlled, especially at the age of 18. Jill married for love, had two children with him and realised in her mid-twenties that life was not going as well as she had wished for. Her husband could be physically abusive, although she said she often felt like she deserved it as she used to goad him so much. The sex was never great, but what bothered her the most was that everything was always someone else's fault. He never took responsibility for anything; even if he didn't want to go out with his mates he would blame her, telling them "She wants me to stay in, so I'd better look after her." Jill couldn't wait for him to clear off out so that she could have some peace!

They tried a number of things to make it work (her parents were still together even though they couldn't stand each other so Jill and her husband felt they were expected to stay together too – how mad is that?) even considering emigrating – as it was obviously England's fault that their life was crap, until one day Jill knew she had to get rid of him. There are two possible scenario's to end this issue – you go or he goes. My mother always said the wisest thing she did when she separated from my father was that she threw him out and kept the property, that way at least we had somewhere to live. Jill took the same approach and he left. What was the straw that broke the camel's back? Jill's husband had a job that he didn't enjoy and kept saying he was going to do something different. Of course, he didn't, what he did was moan about it every day. Jill would ask him the question we all ask our nearest and dearest every day. "How was your day?" His reply, every day was "Same shit, different day." It was that simple repeated phrase that made Jill realise that she needed to get away from him. Meeting someone new also made her realise that there were sunnier horizons out there. These days, many years later, Jill is happily married and living out her dream life with someone she loves and makes her happy. It is possible.

The next tale is of a friend of mine who did something that many women find very hard to understand, she left her husband and her children. She had been married for many years and had grown increasingly isolated from her husband and more aware than ever that she felt like she was dying inside. Not physically, but emotionally, spiritually and sexually. Her husband took little care in his appearance, her sex life was non-existent and the children became the focus of their lives. As so often happens there comes a breaking point although Dee wasn't aware of what it was, all she knew was something had to change. She knew that he was a better carer for the children, as in he was a house husband anyway whilst she went to work. She was struggling to make her business work and it wasn't based on location. It so happened that she got more requests for work from somewhere an hour's drive away so she upped sticks, found a house and found a new life for herself. She would see the children every other weekend and during the school holidays whilst she went away and found herself.

Dee's journey was not an easy one. She struggled with depression, her business folded and she felt increasingly isolated, but slowly she left the shell of her relationship with her husband (who had stripped away her personality and her conscious self) and she learnt to love herself and find out who she was. She also learnt to be a better mum; being with her husband had stopped her from having fun with the children, but her personal journey brought her closer to them and they have thrived. It is not for us to judge someone else's journey although many spend more time doing that than looking at themselves.

Dee also found out who she was sexually; the theme of an unsatisfactory sex life comes up time and again, if you'll excuse the pun. If your wife or girlfriend isn't having sex with you she's not happy with you. That could be because you've upset her in some way, you are slowly doing her head in or because she has found someone else.

This brings me to three tales of people who have left their husbands because of emotional and psychological abuse. All three have a similar type of husband – the subtle controller and all were with them for a long time, the shortest being fourteen years. The women were aged from late thirties to late forties and all had tried to leave their husbands before. It was the control that their men had over their minds that prevented them from leaving. All of them had self-doubt fostered by the same thought implanted in their heads – "You won't find anyone else like me." Not one of them realised the truth in that statement – that was the bloody point, they didn't want anyone like 'you'. What they needed, and what they wanted, was someone else. Something else they all had in common was that they had all had affairs – some longer, some shorter and all reached a breaking point.

Lady number one – Erica. She has a successful career, she was known together with her husband by many people in their peer group and no-one suspected anything was wrong. Erica was a fine actress (as in the front she put on for everyone else) and a dutiful wife. She had been with her husband for more than twenty-five years and had thought about leaving him for at least half of that time. It's a question that comes up time and time again. Why did they wait so long? As someone once said about staff relationships and under-performing staff – there is long term pain and short term pain. Given the choice get it over and done with quickly because either way you're going to feel it so why prolong the agony?

Her sex life had been a constant thorn in her side, he suffered from impotency and although he tried it was a constant disaster. Could anything make you feel less attractive? She found that other men did like her and she had a few affairs over the years, but it was the death of her parents that convinced her it was time to change. She knew she couldn't live a lie any longer. Once the decision was made she was amazed how quickly everything fell into place and a holiday away really helped her to crystalize her plans for the future. Sometimes that break from reality is what is needed to see your future. *Shirley Valentine* wasn't a worldwide hit by coincidence.

Lady number two – Sam. She had wondered why she had ever married her husband; she had been with him five years before they got married, had a child from a previous relationship and had two more with him. She loved her kids, she loved her pets and she loved her friends, but she had fallen out of love with him many years before. She'd tried to leave him on a number of occasions, once even having a house ready to move into, but backing out at the last minute. What kept her there? Two things, the first was his control over her confidence, if someone tells you that they will never get any better than him, if you are told you are stupid, if you are told this is as good as it gets enough times then you can believe it all. Especially if you think that the person who tells you such things loves you and is doing it for your benefit. Reading that from a book makes it sound ridiculous, because it is, but when it is happening to you and it is a constant in your life, that logic becomes your life. It works the same if you have the same internal dialogue; should you consistently tell yourself that you are a pathetic creature that no one else will want then you will become that person.

The second reason for staying was 'for the kids'. One child had already grown up resenting him, and now the other children were voicing their disquiet. What changed her perspective? Her friends had been telling her to leave him for a long time, so had members of her family, but one day someone entered her life who not only changed how she saw the world, but how she saw herself. *Shirley Valentine* again. That made the parting so much easier. The guilt at seeing someone else left her very quickly, her sadness at knowing she would hurt him was overcome by her sense of what was best for herself and the children and her mindset went from what seemed a very difficult decision to a very easy decision in a short period of time.

Trying to control someone by using bullying tactics (psychologically as well as physically) is like trying to hold mud in your hands. The more you squeeze the more passes between your fingers.

Lady number three – Louise. Another long term relationship, another person with no belief in herself, another person who believed her husband helped her and gave her strength – until she left him and realised that he had kept her in a weakened position all the time she had been with him. That's not strictly true, of course, because there is always a time, at the beginning, when love does exist. It might not be ideal, but it is enough to bring two people together. Trying to keep that feeling seems a very difficult thing to do, but it isn't. You just have to go back to the start – something I'll explore in another chapter.

Louise was her husband's second wife, and he had other children from previous relationships; Louise accepted that as we often do when going into a new relationship, we're all grown-ups and realise that our partners have history before us. Louise and her husband had a child themselves and settled into domesticated bliss. After a few years the pair of them started a business together which flourished and grew, bringing with it the advantages of wealth and status. Other people expected certain behaviours and Louise become more aware of her standing in the local community. No breath of a scandal would pass their lips. And so it came to be that Louise's husband used the same techniques as Sam's – "You will never find anyone better than me and who would look at you?" And so on and so on. She left him once and there was a separation of 6 months; he promised to change as he wanted her back and she believed him. He wooed her back and things were different until, inevitably, things went back to the way they were and Louise realised she was trapped.

As she became unhappy she also became more aware of other men and other men became aware of her, but she would not stray until one day something happened. Someone talked about her in glowing terms (none of which she believed), but the effect was what was needed. The affair was short, the friendship remained and she left her husband never to return. It wasn't the affair that gave her strength, it was realising that someone else would want her, that she did have value as a person and that she was being held back and she needed to change things if she didn't want to waste her life.

There will be men reading this who have realised that their wife/partner is acting differently – not in an obvious way, but in subtle changes. There will be women who can relate to one or more of these stories. The question is what will you do? If the man suspects his wife is having an affair then what can he do to win her back? This is what this book is all about. Why would he want to win her back? More importantly how did he lose her in the first place? In self defence people will often ask the question how would they deal with this scenario or that scenario when the most obvious question is how do you avoid the scenario in the first place? To answer this we need to look at the life of the player, the person who will be looking to steal your wife, which is what the next chapter is all about.

For the woman reading this, your choice is simple. Do you stay or do you go? You have to examine why you fell in love in the first place, do you love him now? Do you want to stay with him? Have you fallen in love with someone else? Does life genuinely look better on the other side? These answers come much later, but will be dealt with in depth, first let's talk about 'Alfie'.

Key points to remember:

1 **Trying to control your partner – is it by spending money on them or by coercion?**
2 **Neglect – drifting apart because your attention isn't on the relationship, but is instead on work, hobbies or your friends.**
3 **Five stories:**
   Jill – "same shit, different day".
   Dee – leaving the family home and the children.

Erica – a break from reality pointed to the future
Sam – psychological bullying.
Louise – going back wasn't the answer.

Chapter 3
It began with Michael Caine

That's probably not strictly true, but it does rather seem that way when he made *Alfie* in 1965. *Alfie* was the bench mark for all players, although plenty of British soldiers seemed to think the same was true of the American service men stationed in the UK in the Second World War. With good reason too. Before WWII the female population of Nottingham outnumbered the males by ten to one; after the war was over it had been reduced to six to one. That's a lot of women going overseas and it wasn't just Nottingham that was affected either. The Americans had a lot of things that the British soldier couldn't compete with; money, nylons (stockings), cigarettes, better uniforms and in the run up to D-Day in 1944, plenty of time. Whilst the British soldier was in France, the Far East and North Africa the good looking, smooth talking Yank was in the Home Counties taking a young lady to the movies and afternoon tea. It was an intoxicating picture to the housewife at home with the threat of invasion, bombs and rationing to deal with.

It wasn't all one sided though, the dashing pilots of the RAF, in the wake of the Battle of Britain were also sending the British girls swooning. How could a lowly infantryman or munitions worker compete with the heroes of the sky or the saviours of the Empire? It wasn't easy. Fast forward a few years and the heroes of the services were replaced by guitar players and singers as rock n roll took hold in the mid 1950's. To young girls this was all very exciting; every boy wanted to be in a band, every girl wanted to be with these rebels. The ordinary bloke in the street was having to try harder in every way, often without success. How many of our fathers struggled to get laid and found themselves with Beryl from down the road, the good girl who would make a man happy by marrying our fathers? Unless your parentage was one of the rock n roll rebels or the bad boy that every mother warned your mum to stay away from. And so it has been, since the war, probably before the war and maybe all the way back to Casanova's time. The challenge of keeping your wife or girlfriend away from these bad boys, these sexual predators, these players.

And yet there is one really easy way of stopping your girl being interested. Be interesting! Be fun! Be a sexual god and her best friend. Because if you're not one of these guys will be. It is impossible to have an affair with a happily married, or co-habiting, woman. They are not interested. You can tell who they are because they walk around with "Fuck Off" printed on their forehead. You won't physically be able to see it, but you will be able to feel it. They are the mistress of the icy stare and no matter what you try you won't get through her wall of invisible steel. The other challenge to the player is the woman who understands the game. She has been around a bit, maybe had affairs in the past, been burned or is just savvy enough to know that you don't want her, per se, you just want to get inside her knickers. This woman is not impossible to crack, but will give you a substantial challenge.

For a long time I was a man in love, faithful, loyal and true. The girl I lived with was wonderful, sexually amazing and the most fun a man could have, but as time went on I wondered if I was missing out. At the time I hadn't slept with that many women and I didn't know if there were things going on in the big wide world that I was missing out on. We parted after more than a dozen years because as people we had grown apart; I still respected her, the sex was still there and I still found her attractive, but it was clear that those years from the late thirties to the early forties changed me and changed her too. We parted and went in very different directions. She later became involved with a man who became her husband, my path was totally different.

I had a good friend at the time, who subsequently died a few years after this conversation, who I turned to in order to get my thoughts sorted. It was one of the funniest conversations I've ever had and turned out to be highly prophetic. Names are changed at this point.

"Hey Tony, how are you?" – me

"Good man, how about you?" Tony, ever cheerful.

"I'm ok, but I just called to tell you that me and Hayley have split up," me sounding a little morose.

"That's great news," Tony is all the joys of spring now. "You're going to find out a universal truth."

"Oh yeah, what's that?" say I, not joining in with Tony's enthusiasm.

"You are going to find that there are more women in the world, than you would ever believe, who want to suck your cock," he tells me like he has found the secret to eternal youth. Somewhat ironic considering his future.

"Bugger off," say I, laughing now. "I phoned you up because I was feeling sad."

"Well don't," he said, "I'm telling you it's true."

"Really? How do you figure that?" I ask, completely baffled by this concept.

Having been in a relationship for such a long time I found the idea of anyone else fancying me other than Hayley to be just plain odd. When I started seeing her I was 30, she was 28, she was gorgeous and I had no fashion sense, a bad haircut and glasses bigger than milk bottles. I try and defend myself that it was the fashion of the time, but it must have passed in ten minutes but I kept wearing them for five years. To this day it amazes me that I seduced her, but we were besotted with each other for a very long time.

Coming out of this relationship was both frightening and exciting, in a way that the unknown sometimes is. As to Tony's prophesy I thought he was off his head. And then he started telling me about his adventures in the Dark Side. Tony had been married for 10 years to a nice looking lady, but as happens with life Tony had become bored with his wife and had one aspiration. To sleep with as many women as he possibly could. And it appeared that there was an endless supply of ladies who were happy to make Tony's dream come true. This amazed me. Tony was not the most attractive man you have ever seen. He was tall, bald, overweight with a dodgy goatee, but with a certain charm and he was very funny. He also possessed a decidedly wicked and intelligent brain.

He began his quest as we often do – an internet dating site; except that Tony realised very quickly that the women on these sites were not the ones he wanted to meet. The ones he wanted to meet were on a site called 'Adult Friend Finder'. He told me to take a look, which I did. Or more specifically he told me to look at a lady he had recently slept with – I was surprised how attractive she was – a blonde in a basque and a horny write up. Next he told me another and another. All were attractive and all were interested in only one thing – sex.

Tony described his first experience of meeting someone from Adult Friend Finder. She was a lady in her late 30's, married, bored, blonde and horny. They met in a hotel near the M1, when he got there she was already in the bedroom. He knocked on the door, she called for him to come in and she was lying there, leaning with one elbow on the bed, her head cupped in her hand and smiling seductively. She told him to take his clothes off, they had sex in a perfectly satisfactory way and when they were finished she shooed him away.

"I went back to my car," he told me, "Having had sex with this gorgeous woman and felt like I'd been used," Tony laughed. "I thought I want some more of that."

But that's not the way it went. If you didn't measure up, to what she was looking for, then you were a stepping stone to some holy grail. Tony quickly learnt the game. It wasn't long before he had a veritable harem at his disposal. Tony later had money troubles when his business was failing – I wasn't surprised when I asked how many women he was seeing. His answer staggered me – eighteen! Eighteen I said, how the hell do you see that many?

"Well," he began to explain, "That's spread throughout the month." As if that made any more sense. "I have four that I really like, but the rest I see in rotation."

"But the messaging and emails, or phone calls, that must take forever," I said.

"It can get tricky," he admitted, "And it takes time. Every now and then though I'll have a real blow out." What followed shocked me. I also found it very funny, or perhaps that's just the badness in me.

"The great thing about chain hotels is that you can have them for 22 hours out of 24, so I'll book a local one and make the most of it. I'll get there to check in at 2pm and the first lady will arrive at 2.30pm (I'm thinking "the first lady?"). I'll have my little seduction kit – a bottle of wine, some chocolates and some nice music." He'd moved on since the "wham bam thank you ma'am" scenario of his first liaison.

"We'll spend a few hours together and she'll go about 5.30pm, usually home to her husband who will ask her if she's had a nice day and she'll say yes, it was nice but hard," he chuckled to himself and carried on. "I'll have a bit of a rest, tidy the room, have a shower and then one of my favourites will show up. We'll go for dinner, have a lovely night, go through the card of mad positions and spend the night together. She'll go about 6.30am, in time for her to get to work. I'll freshen up, go for breakfast and lady number 3 will turn up about 9.30am where we will spend a couple of hours together and I'll leave just before 12pm, having had full value for money."

"How do you do it? Don't you get tired? Sore?" I was intrigued.

"I have some Viagra with me, that helps if things are feeling a bit limp."

"And what about the room?" I asked, "Do they offer to go halves or do you pay for it?" Looking back at this question now I can't believe I asked it, but it did give me the biggest surprise of all.

"Oh they all give me half," he laughed. "The room costs £50, or thereabouts and they all give me half."

"So you shag three women and make a profit of £25 into the bargain?" I was stunned.

"Yes," he laughed, "Great isn't it?"

I was dumbfounded, I'd never heard of such a thing. This was my introduction into the world of playing the game, well, not quite, but it was my first person introduction into it. When I was learning NLP I had heard of a guy called Ross Jeffries who had invented a thing called 'Speed Seduction'. Tony had listened to all of his tapes (remember those before the digital world?) and loaned them to me, but prior to this Jeffries had been on one of Louis Theroux's TV shows. He was somewhat sleazy, but also fascinating. What Jeffries had done was use some of the principles of NLP and used them as a way of seducing women. I had to admit I found it fascinating. His idea was that he had always been shy around girls and subsequently ended up with girls who wanted to be his friend because he was a nice guy, but didn't want to go to bed with him. This was not a happy place to be for the teenage Ross, all his friends were getting laid and he wasn't. He started studying NLP and learnt a few principles that he realised would change his place in the world.

One of the first principles was that if you want something then you must go first. It is at this point that the married men (and by married I mean with a long term partner) really need to take notice because this is where you are screwing up big time. By 'going first' I mean have the emotion first. Think about this, you come home every night and your wife doesn't seem overjoyed to see you. Why? Are you giving her the 'same shit, different day' spiel or do you come in fed up from your commute home or moaning about how bad your day was or how you wish you could change your job? If you are, and she's no longer sympathetic, because she's heard this every day for the past three years, then you are getting the emotion you are giving out. Namely frustration, irritation, anger and she is responding in kind. If you want more love in your life then start giving it first. When I see my partner I am always happy to see her. She's gorgeous, we have fun and we spend a lot of time laughing. Of course we are in a good place. When I was doing my NLP Practitioner training Paul McKenna told us to be 'secret agents of change' and what he meant by that was to create the atmosphere that you want around you. If you want more love, then give love, for happiness, give happiness, for frustration, give frustration.

There was one caveat to that. On a previous course McKenna had told people to go out and smile at the general public and see what reaction they would get – and bear in mind this is in London. This guy happily went around smiling at random strangers and he mostly got a smile back in return, however, one night whilst returning home there were a group of West Ham fans who hadn't had the best of results. They were grumbling at their lack of success when one of them looked at our happy secret agent of change. He looked back and flashed them his broadest smile. The response he got wasn't quite what he expected. "What are you so fucking happy about, twat?" Cue quick look at the floor and not as much random smiling. The time and the place are so important!

Back to the point. Ross Jeffries and his speed seduction method. He really thought about this and worked out what women want. It's not hard to research, pick up any women's magazines and you won't have to wait long before you see the 'sex issue'. Men's magazines do it as well now, but in a very different way. Men look at sex (relationships) as a mechanical device (if I do A I will get result B etc), whereas women know it's all in the mind. Emotions hold the key to love, which is pretty bloody obvious if you think about it – try and put love into a logical context. So, Jeffries found that number one on every woman's list of qualities in a man was sense of humour, this was followed by confidence, nice eyes, tight butt, good chest, strong arms and so on. Now as we know there is only so much we can do with physical appearance; it has somewhat fascinated me that two of the world's most beautiful actors – Johnny Depp and Brad Pitt (both now in their 50's) often have straggly beards and look frankly bloody awful. Is that because they want to be judged on more than their looks? Isn't the struggle that beautiful women also have – there is more to them than just their looks – and there Jeffries learned another lesson. Don't do what everyone else does. Tony passed on the same advice about writing a profile on a dating site, be different, be you and don't cut and paste like so many men do, either because they are not creative or because they are lazy.

It is at this point that speed seduction really makes sense. Jeffries is by no means the be all and end all of knowledge on this subject either as there has now sprung up a whole industry of 'pick up artists' (PUA) who are willing to teach their skills to willing men wanting to have sex with beautiful women. I never went on any of their courses, but I did study some of the methodology (a lot of it was already from NLP) and some way into my time of adventuring read Neil Strauss' seminal book on the subject *The Game*. A number one New York Times best seller, if you asked most people in the UK they would never have heard of it and those men who did also did their best to hide its existence from any women they knew. For good reason, but it's also a really good read.

So what did I learn and how did I use it? More importantly how can you use this to either seduce your wife or (if you were so inclined) somebody else's? And ladies, you can now defend yourself against these methods. The next chapter will help to take you on the journey to finding true love, if you haven't already found it, but it will also take you deep into the world of 21st Century dating, a scary place if you haven't been there before.

Key points to remember:

1	**"Alfie" and the players of the past**
2	**Tony, a hotel room and a night of passion – with a difference**
3	**"Speed seduction".**
4	**NLP and dating**

Chapter 4

The journey begins

For me the journey began by chatting with my single friends and looking around social media. At the time Myspace was the number one social media site and you could search for local women on it and you will also find that good looking women usually have nice looking friends. You could have a good look at their profiles (the security settings weren't as tight as Facebooks' are today) and then do what most men don't do. You read their profile and pick out relevant points for conversation. This is still true of dating sites today – read the profile, friend request them and write a pleasant little note. A 'hi' or a 'wink' is lazy and insipid and no woman wants a lazy insipid man. Before you write the first letter though you must take care of your own profile. Forget Facebook for now, let's think about dating sites, even something as blatant as Adult Friend Finder needs some thought. When I tried internet dating I used match.com – for me it really didn't work, but I did make a few friends and getting laid was almost a given.

So, your profile. First of all, your profile picture. For Christ's sake no photos of your car or you with a fish. Think who you are trying to attract, these are good looking, hopefully intelligent women and they are not interested in fish and they are only interested in your car if they mention it on their profile. You have to think of what a woman is interested in, not in what you are interested in. You do have to talk about your interests, but you have to do it in an engaging manner. Let me help you. A little generic how to do it and how not to do it.

"How not to do it" first.

"I've never done this before so please bear with me. I've just come out of a long term relationship, my friends said this would be a good place to meet new people and so here I am. I can be a little crazy, but that's fun isn't it? I love football, my team is Manchester City (Up the Blues). My job is ok, we've all got to work somewhere haven't we? Ideal date would be a lovely lady, a nice restaurant, great conversation and we'll see what happens.

Looking for someone to make me happy again. I look forward to hearing from you."

This would normally be accompanied by a clearly cropped photo that is not of recent vintage or a photo of a bloke next to his car or holding a fish. That may not be true, but it's not far off it.

Let's analyse the ad strictly from a woman's perspective and what she reads. Remember women speak in indirect speech and men speak in direct speech – in this example a man may think he's being honest, a little quirky and is looking to the future. Here's what a woman thinks. This bloke will be talking about his ex a lot (she doesn't want to know), he lacks any creative ideas of his own, he's probably a dick or drinks too much, why would anyone mention football and see what happens? He just wants a shag. This is where sites like Adult Friend Finder score big – at least its honest. Dating sites proclaim to be about finding the ideal partner, but in almost all the dates I had that wasn't the case at all. If ever the term suck it and see were accurate this was it.

So how would I do it? Something like this. "Ah the wonders of internet dating, that place where we put our souls on the line to be swatted and alternately flattered by attention. Where we converse in intelligent conversation, trade stories and experiences and if we're lucky get to meet someone who looks like their profile picture. Some people claim that this is the best way to meet the love of our life. Clearly we must have some faith in the assumption, but most of us have a healthy dose of British cynicism. Who do I want to meet? The adventurer, the music fan, the reader, the woman who has more laughter lines than worry lines, the woman with a past who doesn't carry it heavily on her back and treats each new day as a challenge and goes to bed at night satisfied that she is a little wiser than when she awoke. What do I offer? A willing ear, interesting dates, good conversation, a reasonable shape, I do look like my profile picture, and I will be on time. Unless Boris Johnson takes over the traffic problems for the whole of the UK, in which case I may have to come by bike."

The difference in these ads couldn't be more different. The second one may well alienate some women and that's a good thing; you're not there to appeal to everyone, you are there to find the women who like you. Some women will think you're funny, some will like the cheekiness, but damn near all will see that it is original. So many men cut and paste other men's profiles. Women are not stupid, not the ones you are interested in anyway. They can spot a cut and paste ad a mile away. The other thing to remember is that women get far more views and replies than men. When I was on match.com it was sometimes hard work keeping up with the replies; not because I am a great lothario (although you are reading my book so I do have some success), but because my profile was interesting and I took time to have a good profile photo and a selection of other photos which all showed me in a good light. The internet is full of fake profiles, or profiles where the men aren't all they seem, a woman's job is to wheedle these out and find the genuine guy. And one other point, find an original name. BillyBragg32 hardly inspires conversation, nor for that matter does BridgetJones27 for a woman.

Now your ad is up. You've paid the one month trial price, for Christ's sake don't pay the six month price, you'll never be on there long enough, the most I was on there was two months. That was enough time to realise it wasn't the place I wanted to be. So now what? Now you start searching. Set your distance parameters; I've had friends who travel all over the country looking for their dream woman. The reality is that it is hard enough to find a woman when you see her two or three times a week, but if she lives over 100 miles away then you are limiting your chances of success, unless you want to go into full player mode then this is ideal. You could literally have a different girl every night, sometimes two, or if you are like Tony three. I do have a friend who is seeing 22 women, as I write this book. I honestly don't know how he finds the time to keep up with the correspondence let alone seeing them. Your choice is your choice and remember this book is aimed at many people from the next Don Juan to the husband who wants to keep his wife to the woman who wants to regain the spark in her husband.

Or the woman who wants to understand how the mind of a man works – or for that matter the girl who finds girls interesting, but more of that later. The nature of this part is how to engage, make conversation and stay in touch.

If I were to use this part as a business presentation then it would follow similar lines to getting new customers. I have often said that business is the art of seduction and most business people laugh. That's because most business people (that I meet) are male and don't have a clue about seduction – that's why I wrote the book in the first place. To use the business analogy: You begin with no clients and you want to fill your order book. What inexperienced people do is market their services to everyone; they put ads in Yellow Pages (I know, some people still do this), they set up Google Adwords and Facebook Ads, they print leaflets and do social media marketing. They target everyone because their product is for everyone – they think. These people very quickly run out of money and as often as not go out of business in the first year. This is very much like the beginner in online dating. When the parameters come up on the website they choose a "woman from 18-99 in a 200 mile radius" of where they live. This is the dumbest thing you can do. It is in business and it is in your personal life. You have to decide on who you want to meet, what they look like, what their interests are, age range, ethnicity, height, weight and distance from where you live. You also have to decide what you want from this experience. I went into it with an open mind. One of the reasons that I started online dating was that everyone I was meeting (in the real world if we can call it that) was blonde. They were all lovely, but I wasn't finding the magic connection – that elusive thing we call love. The fact was that since my early days of dating my priorities had changed. When I began dating I was looking for anyone; I knew I favoured curvy, brown eyed brunettes (like the one I'd just left), but I was open to possibilities. In the eighteen months after my initiation into the new world I dated blondes, brunettes and for one memorable evening a red head. I had an eight month relationship that faded when I knew I didn't love her and didn't want to fall into the trap of having a relationship for the sake of it, but mostly I played the game and I was successful through all manner of devices – and this was before I was online dating in its formal sense. I then fell madly in love with a gorgeous brunette and this continued for about two and a half years, but with one distinct problem. We kept splitting up. We would bowl happily along and then she would have a meltdown about something and go off to seek new pastures. It was a painful and difficult time for both of us although the love never ended. Things came to a head when she left me just before Christmas and I went somewhat off the deep end. For the next 8 months or so I was out of control dating many women throughout that time which wasn't good for me and wasn't good for my business as I became more lost and distracted. My first foray into internet dating came towards the end of this cycle after two women I was dating simultaneously (one married, the other separated) met at a coffee shop one Tuesday afternoon and realised both were seeing me. It was not a happy affair. The separated lady never spoke to me again (a great shame as she was lovely and entirely innocent of my regrettable behaviour), the married one instantly forgave me with the idea that she could somehow save me. That didn't work quite as planned either. Or maybe I should stress, quite as she planned.

The great problem with playing 'the game' is that there are players and there are people who don't understand the rules. The biggest players are on the dating sites; that goes for men and women and whilst I don't deny that some people will find their true love online (one of my oldest dearest friends found her husband online and they are tremendously happy together) I didn't even come close. I did find it a tremendous source of willing partners though and all were single, the married women tended to come from real life.

To get back to my point about not spreading your net too far. You need to specify the distance you want to travel, the age range, and in your mind know what you are looking for. I also found that anyone who sent a wink had the tendency to not be the greatest conversationalist, although this wasn't always the case. What I did was put in an age range of 35-52 (I have always preferred younger women), the distance I would travel was 50 miles (although the website insisted on selecting women for me in the Nottingham region – an hour's drive was okay) and I actively sought brunettes, preferably with brown eyes. That's what you have to do, choose what you like and stick to a plan. To use the business analogy again we talk about an avatar – what our ideal customer looks like, their financial buying power, where they live, what car they drive, do they have children? Once we have established that avatar then we know who our marketing is aimed at, where to spend money trying to get those customers and where to look for them. If your avatar drives an Audi A3, lives in a 4 bedroom house with 2-3 children, is happily married and has an income around £50,000 a year you are not going to find that person in the inner suburbs of a major city where people mostly live on benefits and drug crime is rife. I know what you're thinking, you're sitting reading this and saying, "But you can't do that for a person". If you're a woman you're really thinking this because emotions are important to you and looks are not your prime concern. Well, that's nonsense and you're kidding yourself. Have a think, or go onto Google and find photos of the following actors: George Clooney, Brad Pitt, Johnny Depp, Ryan Gosling, Bradley Cooper, Gerard Butler, Leonardo di Caprio or John Goodman. Who do you fancy? In the mystical world of make believe who would you have if you could have anyone? Would any of you wonder what the personality was like of your favourite? Well, yes you would after you had seduced him and left him wanting more. Why would you think that real life is any different? Online everyone is attracted by looks first and personality second. It's how you find someone you want to look at and learn more about. In real life it might be a little different but it is true that someone's personality can make them less attractive as well as more attractive. There are plenty of people who look great but when you talk to them you find that they are not your cup of tea at all. In case you're wondering why I didn't ask the same question of men as to whom they find attractive it always comes down to the same fantasises: Kylie Minogue. Cheryl Cole and for readers of 'Zoo' (a UK men's magazine), Lucy Pinder;

although there is a certain following for Helen Mirren as well. Plus men will readily agree that looks are important.

This process works for whether you are looking for the love of your life or the next notch on your bedpost. The closer the person is to 100% on your list of requirements the more likely you are to find true love. It would be a good idea now to go away and find a piece of paper and describe this woman (or man) in as much detail as you can so that you can stimulate your reticular activating system to find this person. What's that? It's the part of your brain that helps you find what you're looking for. You will be aware of it when you buy a new car – there was time when no one drove the car you bought and now you see them everywhere; you've possibly even seen one parked right next door to yours in a car park or sat behind one at the lights and once there were none there at all. Weird, isn't it?

I first started thinking about what I really wanted in a partner over twenty years ago. I can remember where I was and what I wanted. I wanted a girl with brown eyes (they do something to me even I don't understand), long brown hair, she had to be curvy (I've dated slim girls, but I do love boobs), she had to be interested in history and visiting places, she had to be into physical training (not in a fanatical way, but in a way that showed she cared about herself) , we'd have to share the same sense of humour, she'd need to be no taller than 5' 5", no shorter than 4' 10", she'd have to be ambitious, we would have to be sexually compatible (a list on its own), she would be white or Mediterranean (no not racist, just my preference) and age range came into it too. These days my age range would be 35- 52 – at the time of writing I'm 51, so a 17 year spread. When I first came up with the list I would probably have gone for 23 – 35. I was 29 at the time. Within a year I had met a girl who hit all of these criteria; I have since dated another girl who also fit all of these criteria, but most interestingly the girl I am now in love with hits all of these criteria except she is blonde. This one rather took me by surprise as I've never fallen in love with a blonde before (remember I joined the dating agency because I kept meeting so many blondes), but it turns out she is a natural brunette who dyes her hair. I happen to think she looks better blonde as well, sometimes that happens.

When I began my dating journey I went out with a brunette who also dyed her hair blonde and I really liked it. These days she is back to her natural colour and I still think she suited the lighter colour. Another ex is now blonde and she definitely looked better as a brunette, she had a gorgeous chestnut colour and long hair too. It could be you're reading this thinking no wonder you were dating for so long, looking for Miss Perfect, but that's the choice I made and I am now happier than I've ever been. You can't take the blueprint as gospel though. I also dated a couple of brown eyed brunettes who didn't click sexually or emotionally and both were lovely looking ladies. Looks are the start, but it's the chemical connection that we absolutely crave; that magic that turns lust into love.

Whether in business or love this process works. You can't just keep dating anyone, you have to look for the person who touches your heart, unless all you want to do is to have sex with as many women as possible – and modern life definitely allows for that. Tony's advice to me about how many women wanted to do rude things to me applies for you too. As you'll read in the sex survey women love sex; men might think they are the predators but women leave us for dust.

Back to the method. You have your profile and you are looking through searches. The absolute key thing to remember here is to be realistic. You will see gorgeous women and you will see some you like the look of; you will also have women contacting you (a real novelty at first), some will be nice, some will be ok and some will be fakes. How do you spot a fake? It will only have one photo, perhaps two at most and will say something like Blonde, blue eyes, new to this blah, blah. If you have a look around the dating sites you will see loads of these that are almost the same word for word. The hair and eye colour will be different, but in all other respects they will be fake profiles. Exactly what they are trying to do I'm not sure, possibly extort money from you, I don't know as I never replied. They might also ask for your email address in exchange for 'explicit photos', again it will be a fake profile and should be ignored. They are as fake as those letters from Nigeria telling you that you've won their lottery and all they need are your bank details. Impossible to believe that anyone ever fell for these scams, but they did, they do and don't let it be you. My one attempt at poetry in the whole book.

With that we have got past the fake profile minefield and now you are looking for someone in whose company you would enjoy spending some time. As I said don't get too attached and don't be surprised if you are ignored or if a reply takes a couple of days. The secret to this is to look for 6-12 girls right from the off; it's like a hotel or airline overbooking their capacity. It might happen that all 12 reply, but the likelihood is that 3-6 will and that will give you more than enough to be getting on with.

What do you write in your first message? Anything you like really. Her profile will give you all the clues you need. She will tell her what her interests are, what she is looking for, including her preferences. If she says she is looking for someone 35- 45 and you are 50 don't let that put you off. Start off by acknowledging the discrepancy in age range and then explain why you have written. For example:

"Hello, I saw you wanted someone a little younger than me, but I couldn't resist your profile when I saw that you are interested in the books of A A Milne/Egyptian pharaohs/the handbags of Prada. I really hope you don't mind me writing to you." Explain why you share the same interests and at the worst she might say "I'm sorry but I am really strict on my age ranges because ....", if that's the case you've lost nothing but tried. However, what normally happens is that you start up a conversation. Imagine yourself at work and you overhear a girl talking about a subject you also have an interest in. You would, just out of interest say ""wow, I so rarely hear of anyone who is interested in the films of Joe Dante (any subject remember), which is your favourite? (Out of interest, in case you have no idea who he is, he directed the first *Gremlins* movie, although others may like

Innerspace or *The Howling*). The chances of this happening are minuscule, but at least now you will know. Back to the point; what you wouldn't say do is talk about your age first, you would just engage in conversation; the rules are slightly different on the internet, but the rule remains. To get a conversation going you must first speak, everything after that is feedback. If she converses fully you've done a great job, if you don't hear much back you're not her type. You really have to get used to being rejected on the internet – it's not real rejection, it's based on looks or those early exchanges. What will make you stand out from the crowd is by (a) reading her profile and being able to talk about things on it and (b) that men are unbelievably bad at communicating online with women. I base this purely on personal experience and feedback from other internet daters.

Most men can't follow a simple line of conversation and your ability to do this will make you stand out from the crowd. The absolute no-no of internet dating is to mention sex before the woman does. Some women will talk about sex quite early on, some will give you their phone number and some will send you provocative photos; in this case you will follow their lead. You will almost certainly be sleeping with this woman within seven days of first contact. Most women are not like this though and you have to coax their information from them. Women are usually garrulous on the internet and will chat about lots of things. The key to this is move the level of conversation on quite early, if you really like them. You don't want to be over eager, but equally remember they are talking to as many, if not more, people than you and your job is to reduce that number so they are interested in you. Do you see the business comparison again? In a crowded marketplace as a business you are trying to get your message heard. It is exactly the same in internet dating and the way to do that is to be honest and sincere.

Another way to do that is to get the girl away from the mentality of the site i.e. trying to answer lots of men whilst talking to you. The best way of doing this is to start conversing either by text or email. She will only do that if she trusts you; I have quite a good presence online so if I liked a girl I could point her at my website to prove I was who I said I was. Remember, there are fake men as well as fake women online. If the conversation is tripping along nicely you should have a phone number or email address in a day or two, sometimes it comes earlier, but beware of anyone overkeen, they may also wish to boil your rabbit too. Once a phone number is received things really pick up a pace then. If you have "WhatsApp" on your phone this is a great way to contact each other; for a start all the messages are free and if you have a kinky girl it's much easier to send photos. What do you send if she asks for one of you? For some reason women always send 3 photos at least to every one you send of yourself. I think it's because their bodies are far more interesting, but who knows? Which leads us to the 'cock photo'. Should you ever send one? The answer lies completely in the girl – she may love them and will ask for one, but most women don't and to send one unsolicited is the biggest mistake any man can make in online dating and yet I hear of it all the time. Yes women love sex, yes they might like the male appendage, but they don't want random photos of an erect penis unless they ask for it. And then what? Should you? What if you think she will laugh at it? This comes down to your vanity and getting the right angle. A 'cock photo' from the wrong angle will make you look like a 6 year old boy, get it right and it may have the desired effect!

However, we move on slightly too fast. Assuming the lady is not a collector of said photos you will need to meet with her and we come back to the point I made earlier – coffee shops are the best. Low risk level, easy escape for both of you (in a polite manner) or you can hang out as long as you like or as long as your tolerance to caffeine or your wallet can stand it.

It is at the point of meeting that your role as a seducer now comes into play. First of all the only emotion you must show upon seeing her for the first time is happiness; this is much easier with some ladies than others but no matter what, utter disappointment or exuberant joy, always remain the gentleman. This is all part of the act remember, you must act in a certain manner to achieve the result. Of course, you could take on any persona. In *The Game* Neil Strauss took on the name 'Style', one of his contemporaries was 'Mystery'. These guys took the art of picking up women to a whole other level, but they came to the same conclusion I did, although I reached it much sooner, sex can become boring if it is soulless. Yes, I know, you're thinking but the point is to get laid as much as possible. Well maybe, it really depends on your mind set. The real name of this game is to sleep with someone you want to sleep with, not merely a challenge. Did I ever regret any of the liaisons I had? A few, but not many when I look back. All, without exception, were lovely. Not all were honest as to their intentions – or maybe I didn't measure up – but all were delightful company. Whether as a one night (or afternoon) stand or a relationship i.e. something that went on for a while. Some men are straight up and tell a lady that she is not the only person in their life, I left it open, they didn't ask me and I didn't ask them. The exception to this was the relationships I had during this time, although some of those I couldn't claim to be faithful in. If we think that some of these ladies were married as well we were as bad as each other, if someone were to judge us.

Which brings us to morality. The previous chapter began with tales of 'Alfie Elkins', the fictional character created by Bill Naughton, played brilliantly by Michael Caine and very differently by Jude Law. One set in 1965 and the other in 2004. In those dividing years it was clear that there had been a sea shift in the way the "jack the lad" was seen. Don Draper, the womanising character in *Mad Men*, the TV series about advertising executives epitomised the attitude of the 1965 *Alfie*. Don is good looking, charming, wealthy and has a high sex drive; it fuels his creativity. Whilst the Michael Caine character is a lot more down to earth he is no less successful. The characters prove that women fall for good looking, charming men, in much the same way that men fall for sexy, drop dead gorgeous girls. In the 60's if a girl acted in the same way that Draper or Alfie did she would be vilified and thought of as a 'slut'. Fast forward to the 21st Century and a woman who has had a number of sexual partners is not seen in the same way. Billy Connolly once summed it up nicely when talking about religion.

"How many virgins do you get for being a suicide bomber. Is it 70, 20, 40, 53? That's when you know the number has been decided by a committee. Can you imagine it? 53 virgins! The very thought of 53 fucking virgins is a nightmare! It's not a prize, it's a punishment! Give me 2 fire breathing whores any day of the week!!"

He has a point. Can you imagine teaching a virgin? That might be all right when you are teenagers, but if you are in your thirties or forties, or older, you want to be on the receiving end of someone who has half an idea what they are doing. Equally it would be nice if you knew what you were doing too.

So as a man we want a woman who knows what she's doing, we want someone who will be an absolute slut for us, a porn star, but we hate the idea that she has done this with anyone else. What the hell is that about? Tony Curtis had an interesting attitude to sex (bearing in mind he slept with most of the beautiful women of the time, including Marilyn Monroe). His view was "Once it's over it's only an orgasm." What is it that convinces us that monogamy is the natural order of things? Obviously it is religion and our upbringing.

"Thou shall not commit adultery" is the sixth commandment. The last is "Thou shall not covet," which can mean someone else's wife as well as their life or belongings. We are taught this from an early age, that it is wrong to commit adultery, but I have done it many times and mostly without guilt. As I said once before you cannot have an affair with a happily married woman and if you are having an affair you are probably making her happy. What happens with that affair is up to you two, but if you end up together and the husband (or if you are a woman reading this, the wife) is left on her own then they neglected the person enough for them to want to stray. It is possible that the partner is the innocent party and the person committing the adultery is just a bastard or a bitch, but in my experience this was not the case.

When I began this journey some seven years before this book was written my thought was that you only slept with one person at a time, as in who you were seeing. This led to some very tempting situations where my long term partner wanted me to sleep with her and I wouldn't because by that time I was seeing someone else. That attitude changed in time and it wasn't unknown for me to see two ladies in a day, occasionally one leaving only thirty minutes or so before the next arrived, but they were my crazy days. Turn the clock back seven years and I would have taken up the offer and it could have changed the course of my life. Such is the benefit of hindsight. When I was seeing so many women at the same time did I have any thoughts of guilt? The answer was 'no', however, as time went on and the relationships came to an end I did hate hurting people and when someone tells you that they love you and you can't reply the same back, that isn't nice.

So why no guilt? Because I wasn't in love. Some of the ladies I was seeing were playing the same game, some were married and some in relationships anyway, but I wasn't playing the monogamy game. I liked them all, but wasn't in love. Sometimes I'd see someone, know she was going back to her partner and there I was still on my own. It gets to the point where it all becomes pointless and that's when I got out of the crazy cycle and started to look for someone to be with. Love truly is the answer, but whilst you don't have the answer sex, dinner, the movies, cuddles and great conversation is a worthy substitute.

If you've been sitting there reading this and getting more and more annoyed with me ask yourself this, how do you know your partner/wife/husband isn't having an affair? In 1948 Alfred Kinsey published his report on *Sexual Behaviour in the Human Male*. It revolutionised the way sexual behaviour was seen. Homosexuality, extra marital affairs, masturbation, bestiality, all were subjects explored for the first time and it was a runaway bestseller. Kinsey was feted from on high and the Kinsey organisation was seen as a bastion of knowledge on sexual behaviour. It was ground breaking information at a time when sexual education was in its infant stages. It also led to *Sexual Behaviour in the Human Female* in 1953 – this was an even bigger shock to the system. It caused so much controversy that Kinsey was reviled by the Establishment. In his excellent biography of Kinsey, Jonathon Gathorne-Hardy writes "The American public had just been able to take Kinsey's terrible language about the appalling activities of men, about American womanhood they could take neither the language, nor the activities. American womanhood masturbating, having orgasms, pre-marital sex, extra-marital sex, sex with each other … This simply could not be American womanhood. Kinsey had clearly confined his enquiries to prostitutes.

All over the country the churches rose in fury. Catholics, Kinsey had expected, but now Protestants were equally furious."

It didn't affect sales though, the Female volume sold even faster than the Male version. It sold 185,000 copies in two years and sold as many copies in total in two years as the Male version sold in six. It wasn't only the USA where the book sold, with interest coming from all over the world. Which sort of sums up the problems that people have with sex; many people are fine with hearing about it as long as it doesn't happen to them.

Many men who read this book won't believe that their wife has ever had an affair or would never have one. They also won't believe that they will be interested in other women, threesomes, sex clubs and even I was surprised by this one, prostitution. I have a very good friend, a lady called Becky Adams, or Madam Becky as she was known for many years, and she knows all there is to know about prostitution having run brothels in the Milton Keynes area for twenty years. She has been a great sounding board for this book and we were talking about the girls one day. My question was "How do the girls cope if they become involved in a relationship?" Becky's answer really surprised me.

"Lots of the girls were in relationships."

"And their partners knew?" I asked.

"No, not at all, That was frowned upon by the other girls. If the other girls knew that a bloke knew their wife or girlfriend was on the game they didn't like that at all," Becky explained. "What happened was that the girls would do their shift whilst their bloke was at work."

This is what else she told me. Most men who use prostitutes do so because they can't get what they want at home and that can be for many reasons:

1 Kissing – men want to be kissed and complain that their wife/partner doesn't do this. Which is weird one as many wives complain that their husbands or partners don't kiss either! Perhaps it would help if the two talked to each other. For those who have been brought up on the understanding that prostitutes don't kiss this is quite a revelation. Well they do and men like it.

2 Hobbyists – this came as a total revelation to me. There are men whose hobby is sleeping with working girls; that's what they call them as well, not prostitutes. There is even a website (there would be wouldn't there) where men compare different girls, rate them and recommend them. It's called 'Punternet' if you're interested and a fascinating insight it is too. It is also interesting to understand that some men don't consider this cheating; for them it is sex, but without any form of commitment and therefore, not cheating on their partner. I can think of a lot of ladies who would be bothered by the cost as well as the fact that they were sleeping with another woman. An interesting, if perhaps expensive, hobby.

3 Pay to walk away – this is more for single guys who just want sex and no emotional attachment. A cheaper way of doing this is by becoming a player, but it could be that they don't want to learn how to do that.

4 Speciality – this is particularly helpful to the man who cannot tell his wife or partner about his fetish. The things that Becky described were adult babies, the puppet fetishists, the men who wanted to be dominated and the role players. A quick look into each of these: first of all the adult baby's, these are men who dress in nappies, will suckle on a lady's breast as if feeding, be put to bed in a cot and generally treated like a baby. I don't claim to understand it, but this is what turns them on. The puppet fetishists are the men who like to be masturbated by a fur puppet in the hand of a girl until they orgasm; the puppet would then be put in the washing machine for future use. Becky said they had a fur monkey and a Sooty puppet that did the job very well. Men who want to be dominated – very common, but not so much so in brothels as there is such a healthy BDSM scene in the outside world. Men would asked to be tied up, gagged, beaten and generally controlled to get themselves off. Finally role players, these would be men who would want the girls to dress up as nurses, in massage gear (an easy one in a massage parlour), air stewardesses, police woman, anything that could be found at a local fancy dress shop. All of these things were usually kept from wives or partners for fear of their partner/wife being repulsed or rejecting them.

5 The two for one, or three for one guys. These are men who want to explore the fantasy we discussed earlier i.e. two or three girls and one guy. Becky said she would do a pick n mix in times like these. Sometimes a couple of guys and half a dozen girls "We'd throw a fat one in for free," she said! Of course it cost a bit more (for the numbers, you're not priced based on weight), but the fantasy was indulged. There are also organised sex parties, in a similar fashion to the 'real people' sex parties. Becky was of the opinion that these were nowhere near as much fun and the guys who went in for them had no respect at all for the women involved. Respect when talking about a working girl seems a bit strange, but they are human as we all are and a polite customer was always treated better than a rude or obnoxious one.

6 Older gents and the disabled. Both of these have their own particular needs. I read about the life of a prostitute many years ago; I can't remember the title now, but she did say that giving an old guy a blowjob can give you jaw ache. It's often forgotten that both older people and the disabled still have physical needs which have to be addressed and working girls can help with this.

That sums up the reasons why men visit working girls, or have them visit them. Women do use escorts, but in nowhere near the numbers that men do. I have heard of women wanting threesomes and they would hire a girl rather than it being someone they know or going through the internet channels. That element of the girl walking away and reducing the moment when it is all over and what do you do with the third person?

For some prostitution is not their way, they would prefer the 'speed seduction' method, but in all honesty most men, and women, just want a relationship with someone who they can get along with, share their lives and have a great sex life and from there anything is possible. Marriage, children, great holidays, building a business or simply having a great life together. It is from these seeds that a life is made, most journeys of the relationship kind begin with a kiss, but if you are going down the internet route get the profile and pictures right. If your relationship starts with a meeting at work or on a night out, the message is pretty much the same: good communication and treat each other well. If you're not ready for that there is always a visit to the local brothel which could keep you going too.

Now we come to the part of the book where the ladies I have spoken to tell us what they need from men, it begins in the next chapter with how they would like you to look and in the following chapter what they like in the bedroom. I hope you find it illuminating.

Key points to remember:

1   **Internet dating – sorting your profile.**
2   **Who you are looking for, who is your ideal partner?**
3   **Writing the first messages.**
4   **Morality**
5   **Alfred Kinsey and his landmark books on human sexuality (1948 and 1953).**
6   **Prostitution and why men pay for them.**

Chapter 5
The grooming survey

Early on in the gestation of this book I put a male grooming survey on Facebook and received back a wealth of replies. I did consider posting them all, but you quickly see the trends so this is what I am going to share with you. I'm also including some of the replies that I thought were particularly amusing including a section from a group of widows who were clearly enjoying themselves far too much.

This was how I sent out the survey: "Thank you for agreeing to help with this. I am writing a book on relationships and I think that male grooming is an area that should be covered. Who better to ask than women? All replies are 100% confidential.

Males grooming – a simple survey

1   Clean shaven, stubble or beard?
2   What is your favourite male body spray – does anyone like Lynx?!
3   Your favourite attire on a man (given the understanding of work environment)
Suit and tie; jeans and t-shirt; smart casual; Bermuda shorts and Hawaiian shirt? What works for you – any or none of the above.
4   Underwear – boxers, Y-fronts, slip briefs etc?
5   Hair – long, short. Medium, bald?
6   Body hair – chest hair - yes or no?
Under carriage: Natural, trimmed, shaved?
7   Body – toned, muscular, regular, skinny?
8   Anything else you'd like to add?"

The replies:

Question 1: Clean shaven or stubble? This was definitely a 50-50 reply. Some ladies love stubble, some prefer clean shaven. A couple of the more indepth replies:

"I like a little stubble, I'm not into pretty guys"

"Depends on the person - but never a beard. I would say 50/50 clean shaven vs stubble." *I found this reply interesting as in 2014, when this book was written, the beard is making a huge comeback. It's almost like the 1970's out there, but do women like it?*

"Hard, I like them all, I have always gone for a guy with stubble, but married a man with a beard. It depends on the man, not all men suit beards or stubble and some just look wrong without!" *That seems to be a concise answer to the question.*

"Clean shaven but obviously can't expect a man to shave every day, same as a woman they can't shave sensitive areas every day" *There's a lesson there I'm sure!*

"Clean shaven (if you're talking about the face). Anywhere else, beard." *Following a theme! See question 6.*

Question 2. *I was joking about Lynx so I was surprised how many women like it!* What is your favourite male body spray – does anyone like Lynx?!

"Love CK One on a man, but anything fresh smelling including Lynx?!"

"Lynx Excite is my fave but Le Male EDT is the best"

"I loved Lynx Atlantis. Not sure on body spray but the original Joop is a very horny smell. Paco Raban ultraviolet is stunning so is Versarci Eros." *This is someone who knows her smells.*

"I don't like Lynx, smells cheap and boyish - Prefer aftershave like Fahrenheit and most come with their own body spray." *I have to admit I'm confused by this reply, does she mean men have their own smell, she can't tell what they smell of or is she being rude?*

"Lynx is good, anything as long as it's not too overpowering." *A definite lesson here.*

"Does anyone like Lynx?! I don't care less as long as they don't smell of body odour." *Another lesson well worth heeding.*

"CK One, Davidoff, etc varies but NOT lynx, brut, old spice" *Back goes the 70's!*

"No idea - can't smell" *One of my favourite replies.*
"Less is always more!"
"CK One or Paco Raban (which makes me go weak at the knees). Can't stand cheap body sprays they smell like fly killer!!"
"None of them, as they make me cough and wheeze!!"

Question 3: Your favourite attire on a man (given the understanding of work environment)

> Suit and tie; jeans and t-shirt; smart casual; Bermuda shorts and Hawaiian shirt? What works for you – any or none of the above?

The answer to this was very mixed with no clear favourite. Jeans and a nice shirt were mentioned a lot, as was a good suit. Only one person thought the James Bond-dinner jacket look was the best look and another loved uniforms. Football shirts are a big mistake, unless you are playing football.
"Suit, well fitting, nothing cheap and nasty, looks good" *You've been told!*
"Smart casual (though none of the above would apply also at times!)"
Shoes were also mentioned quite a bit, from women? Who would have guessed? Good shoes are a must, but lots of ladies in the survey also like Converse.

Question 4: You now have your clothing sorted, but what do women like underneath? As with every question they knew exactly what they want. The choices: Underwear – boxers, Y-fronts, slip briefs etc? Calvin Kleins were really popular, boxers on the whole, but tight boxers, not baggy. Girls like to see what the package holds before they take a look inside.
"Calvins or commando"
"Boxers - including novelty ones"
"Trunks like the ones David Beckham wears!!"
"I like clean tight boxers nothing baggy with holes in!"
"Boxers - pants are a no no"
"Tight boxers and something nice inside!"
"I don't mind as long as they are clean and changed at least daily!"

"Boxers others are for men in their 80's"

"Undies; A tricky one!! Depends on age and body shape. Young and buff hipsters, don't mind bright colours but NO cartoon prints please. The older man who is in good shape hipsters or A-front in dark colours (CK are the best). Older and fat? Couldn't give a flying fuck because I have no intention of looking!"

"Boxers/jockeys only. Briefs are for girls, Y-fronts for your dad."

This goes to show that you really do have to put the effort in. No more Monday to Friday pants or those with the Superman logo on them. You might have done everything right, but if your trousers come off and the wrong underwear is looking back at her the chances are that you will be out the door quick as you like.

Question 5: Hair – long, short. Medium, bald?
Almost unanimous. Short hair won by a mile, medium was accepted and so was bald. Only one person liked long hair and this lesson from one lady:

"Hair – , short. Or bald (but if balding accept it either trim it short or shave it - NO comb overs!)"

I think we all knew it anyway, but women confirm it. Comb overs and the Bobby Charlton look is the worst ever. I used to have a friend, many years ago, with the longest comb over ever. When he got hot his whole scalp would move like it was on a hinge. Hilarious – and even he had a girlfriend!

Question 6: Body hair – chest hair - yes or no? Under carriage: Natural, trimmed, shaved?

There wasn't a question which elicted more opinions than this one. Everyone had their say on this, and although these are some of the funniest answers there was no universal agreement on pubic hair length. A lot liked the trimmed look, some wanted the shaved approach and some liked natural, although everyone agreed too much hair was a bad thing and very off putting.

"Chest hair yes, downstairs, trimmed or shaved, nothing worse than natural or unkempt! You didn't mention back hair or nasal or ear hair! All should be groomed!"

"Both hairy and smooth are acceptable. The Chewbacca look isn't"

"Hairy, but not a monkey"

"I love chest hair but hair in other areas needs to be trimmed! No hairy ears, nose or uni brow and I need to see what's going on downstairs not be needing a machete!"

"Manscaping is a must"

"Body hair – chest hair - yes in moderation or shaved but no monkeyman! Under carriage: Natural or trimmed, but again not wild and woolly"

"Under carriage - most seem to be shaven which is odd, but ok - but prefer natural."

"I like a bit of chest hair, I also like smooth chests, not keen on gorilla men, too much hair, especially on the back is a bit of a turn off. By under carriage I assume you mean pubes! Do men really shave, shave their pubes?! No I don't think so - as nature intended is fine by me."

"Chest hair is ok. I hate back hair and hair that hangs out of ears and noses and odd ones out of eyebrows !!! Under carriage has to be well groomed not looking like an overgrown bush!!!!"

"Body, like a bit of chest hair, back hair makes me throw up. Under carriage; trimmed or shaved. Do not want to see a jungle down there; something could be living in it."

"Only ever seen natural undercarriage! But I suppose a trim wouldn't go amiss."

"Under carriage shaved or trimmed – no Afros!"

Question 7: Body – toned, muscular, regular, skinny?

On the whole women like a man that is toned, not over muscular. Body building types have a limited appeal and no one in the survey liked a skinny man. Some preferred a little podge, or cuddly as some of them put it, but this lady seemed to nail all the opinions in one sentence.

"Not skinny - I make it rule not to date men who weigh less than I do. It's just demoralising otherwise. If a guy wants to be toned that's fine by me, but as I don't have the perfect body, I don't expect my man to."

Question 8: Anything else you'd like to add?

If ever there was an open question this was it and women know exactly what they want:
"Nails kept nice, no tats, never fake tan..."
"Absolutely no skinny jeans, crocs, speedos or fake tan"
"Every man looks good in a dinner suit. Smell is a big turn on, I've been known to follow a guy round Tesco because he smelt so good. Male grooming is good, men should look after themselves but not in an obvious Joey Essex kinda way."
"Masculine not feminine ..... Good manners ...... I don't like men that pamper themselves but they need to have some self respect and look after themselves. (Good at DIY is always a bonus)"
"Tattoos and a real bad boy"
"No man should spend longer than me getting ready! 5mins in the shower is long enough... Unless you're sharing the shower water of course!!!"
"Must have filed finger nails, no bitten ones and wear proper shoes, trainers for the gym only. Definitely no football shirts."
"For me it all boils down to that something. Something must drag my attention and hold it. If you stand out in a crowd and I don't mean cuz you're the funkiest in there. I mean there has to be something about you, it's different in every relationship I have had. Eyes are massively important."
"Personality is more important than body shape, but if I was having to pick it would be toned I don't find bulging muscles attractive, Personal hygiene is important someone who bathes regularly and makes an effort with themselves is good. Nice teeth are a must. I'm not talking superstar teeth, but someone who brushes and flosses and doesn't have teeth like council

fence posts! Also a big must is clean finger nails I would never get intimate with a guy with dirty fingers!"

"Nice teeth, sexy eyes and a few tattoos can be hot, but depends on the type of person."

"Oral hygiene - must be good. Nails, clean and not bitten. Nice, clean shoes!"

"Teeth! Nice teeth and pleasant breath"

"Personality is the most important thing, along with the way they look at you. All the rest is immaterial!"

"No excessive swearing, politeness at all times (manners cost nothing!) Personally don't like excessive tattoos, no stale body odour, clean teeth a must"

"Being fun, intelligent and lovely more important than all the above"

"Actually made me laugh doing this. Bet I never find a man who meets all of those!"

"The voice, super important - I could never fall for a man with the wrong voice or an awful accent. I love many accents but Scouse or Mancunian is a real turn off."

"A real turn off is a bloke who spends more time getting ready than the female."

"I hate blokes that have long nails and dirty nails biggest turn off. And have to clean their teeth as bad breath a no no .... Thanks for making me think I have OCD in this area as I wish blokes would understand if we do all areas then so should they hahaha."

"I cannot stand macho crap. If a man has a hobby great but not if they are obsessed ...Martial arts, I train five days a week and can't drink or eat filth type guy! Polite with manners and actually being a bit feminine. Just looking and smelling clean. Taking an interest and not speaking to you like you're some kind of meat!"

"What really pisses me off is when you go out and see women who have made a real effort and their man looks like a tramp. Very rude and disrespectful. She has tried her best to look good but he couldn't care less. How would he feel if she went out in joggers, t-shirt and unwashed hair?

Drives me effing mad. And yes I have a husband who sometimes does that."

"I like humour but NOT behaving like a child. I personally don't like short guys ..feel more secure with a taller guy—protected. Size in a willy DOES matter.. not massive, but not less than 6 inches but wide is good. Shoes are essential. They give a lot away about a guy. Accents as well. I hate broad accents ie Brummy, South Yorkshire, Glaswegian."

"I get disturbed if a guy has more toiletries than me & my girly housemate put together....."

Key points to remember:

1　　**Clean shaven vs stubble: 50-50**
2　　**Lynx is more popular than I thought, but overall a bit of money spent on a nice smell is appreciated**
3　　**All sorts of looks are appropriate at given times, except football shirts!**
4　　**Underwear – boxer briefs are the preferred look.**
5　　**Hair – short was by far the most popular style, in this survey at least.**
6　　**Hair on the chest, or anywhere else, should be kept under control!**
7　　**Toned is the favoured look.**
8　　**Nice teeth, nice shoes, fresh breath and don't take longer to get ready than your girl.**

Chapter 6

The sex survey

Having talked about Alfred Kinsey and the impact that his sex studies had on the world I wanted to see what women of the 21st Century were doing. I didn't have the resources or the time that Kinsey had at his disposal so I started with a very simple format. At first I asked some ladies I knew if they wanted to talk about their sex lives, some did and some didn't. A couple of those early interviews are included and then as we talked I realised certain themes were repeating and I worked out the sex survey that is now before you. Everyone answered the same questions and although I know who replied, for the sake of confidentiality all the identities are hidden. What follows is both interesting, enlightening and I hope that you will find it fascinating. Romance is also mentioned and that is a theme which I will examine later on in the book. I wanted to start with one of the first interviews I did. It is quite short, but it will give you an idea of how the survey came about.

Miss AB:
"I am very adventurous when it comes to sex. I love anything and everything that is possible. The only thing I really don't like is anal sex, that hurts and any woman who says it doesn't is an alien. I'm very different to my partner, although when he is in the right mood he is on my wavelength, but I like to take it to the next level.
I love being blind folded and tied up which he used to do, but that stopped a couple of years ago; I have no idea why. That's why I had an affair because the guy I was seeing was up for doing the same as what I liked and was sex mad like me.
I would have sex with two women, but I'd probably be more up for it after I've had a drink as that is when I turn into a horny bitch.
Things I wouldn't do. Go to an orgy; I would worry what I would catch. Oral turns me on the quickest. I love being touched, licked, sucked and fucked over and over again. The gentle side of sex is really important, especially when you are in love. It feels amazing and the closeness is mind blowing and it makes you feel special and loved.
The best sex I've had: sex with my partner, despite his low sex drive we have had hot, wild sex. 2 The affair I had, really good sex in the shower followed by being tied up. 3 With a girlfriend and her fella – now that was something else, he has the best tongue ever!! 4 Just us two. My girlfriend and me, vodka and ice, absolutely amazing.

Sex with a woman feels different obviously, but it's the thought and thrill that it's a woman. I love licking a girl, it is a massive turn on, but I also get as much pleasure giving as receiving.

Threesomes are great, but I've never really given it a second thought about foursomes so it doesn't bother me."

From those simple beginnings came the questions that I asked twenty or so women. To include all the answers would be tedious rather than interesting and what I want to achieve from this survey is for you to learn what goes on in bedrooms, living rooms and bus shelters all over the UK and undoubtedly all over the world. Every word repeated here is true and you might find yourself enthralled, shocked, surprised or possibly even aroused. I have assigned each lady a letter, so if you want to read the survey all the way through from one viewpoint you can or you can follow the questions through in chronological order. Time to let the ladies speak.

1 What is the biggest fault that men have with trying to turn on a woman?

A   *The biggest fault is communication mainly. Men think with their dicks. They think sex is all about coming instead of the basics like seduction, romance and caressing*

B   Trying too hard, doing what they think a woman wants them to do.. ie oral, asking if they are doing it right. Talking too much .

C   *Going too fast - thinking a quick snog and a finger prod count as foreplay!! The way I look at it is this. Men can get from 0 to sex in seconds - for women it takes a little longer. Our bodies have more to cope with. So I either need to be brought slowly to the boil or kept on a permanent simmer. No point in whacking it in if it's not ready to take it !!*

D   For me, men's biggest fault trying to turn women on is that they expect instant results. In my view women take time to warm up. Men on the other hand seem to be able to flick a switch and they are ready to go. Women want to be seduced slowly with cuddles, kisses and exploring each other's bodies.

E   *Not taking their time, kissing, touching, caressing, slowly to ignite the passion and arousing..*

F   Just kissing a woman isn't enough to get her in the mood. A man needs to take his time and really have fun with his woman, make sure she's relaxed and up for it!

G   *Treating us with kid gloves and not showing us that they find us attractive.*

2   What makes a good lover?

A   A good lover is someone that takes time to set the scene. Allow a woman to relax and know it takes more time for a woman to climax than a man. Find out what turns a woman on, again it's communication. Also someone that knows how to kiss a woman sensually.

B   *Someone who is confident in the bedroom. Knows what they are doing. Doesn't ask if they are doing it right. Lets a woman please them too.*

C   A good lover listens to their partner, reads the signs, takes note of what turns them on and what doesn't. A willingness to talk about sex and keeping an open mind re new ideas is good. Also patience, stamina and wanting to please.

D   I adore giving pleasure and it's nice if your lover feels the same.

E   *I can't honestly answer this, I don't know - it is what is acceptable to you at the time. I like to be pampered. I also like to give.*

F   Good lover... Being thoughtful and taking the time to do the above...

G   *A man that's willing to listen and try different things. Case in point: Me 'Darling, slow down, a little gentler, please.' Him 'What? My last girlfriend liked it this way.' Oh dear......*

3   Do you think men listen, or care, enough in the bedroom?

A   Lol think I answered that question in first two. No! Men just want one thing and it doesn't concern the woman .

B   *Some do. Some don't. Depends on the guy you are with.*

C   I think men can get lazy in bed. What woman wants a quick fuck and then sees her loved one roll over and sleep? This, I think, links into what I said earlier re women needing warming up. I think a lot of men can't be bothered with loads of foreplay.

D   *Overall, no. My partner and I have a relationship agreement. Basically we have regular sex(5-7 times a week)however for him, its the physical release, for me I would like for him to be a bit more tender and attentive.*

E   From my personal experience it takes time to learn about each other's likes, dislikes and needs... Some men can lie there and receive, but don't understand it takes time for a woman to get into the 'zone', that we take longer and they don't have the patience. They can sometimes think they must do things harder and faster, when that in fact that can totally be the opposite to what's required.

F   *Not always.*

G   In general, no. They are obsessed with orgasms - theirs and mine, and forget that the journey there is often more important.

4   What have been your top 3 sexual experiences?

A   First a man hit my spot albeit it took a while, but he never stopped until I was happy and it really took me somewhere I had never experienced before, that was selflessness. Secondly, was a long time ago when the first real man I had sex with showed me how to please myself and helped me grow sexually. Thirdly, being tied to a bench and blindfolded and having 3 men take charge and not knowing who was doing what. This was at someone's house, so it was a controlled environment. It ended really when we were all satisfied and nobody came on me, it was all in condoms. It was quite a good experience, I guess the blindfold made it that because the not seeing and not knowing what was happening. You are just left with your imagination and that can go wild if you let it. I guess what I am trying to say is that my imagination is what helps me, not so much the experience.

B   *All night sex. Moved to the jacuzzi then more sex which included anal.. It was none stop and hard. All over the house, sex in the bath then being tied to the bed legs and arms. A threesome with 2 men.*

C   My top sexual experiences all relate to the same man. He was ten years older than me and I was in my teens. He was very experienced; it was the first time I had oral sex, different positions and places. He was very considerate and had amazing stamina. I've measured everyone since against him and no one has come close.

D   *a) Being chosen to be a submissive for a dom. A role I had for 4 years. b) Being fisted - it's an amazing feeling, very euphoric and gives you a high. It's a very long process and needs to be done with care. The power of the body and mind at that time is intense and it is a time where aftercare (cuddles and comfort) is a must.(c) The threesome was planned and was with my dom and his friend. No alcohol was involved (it rarely is in Dom/sub situations). It was a pleasure to give and receive. We met up several times, each with a different theme or aim. It was such a learning curve for me.*

E   This is a hard one..... But if honest, one with a long term 'friend' when I was separated, I was helped to overcome my inhibitions and learn how to just receive and just enjoy, it blew my mind and he taught me so much.

Next one, meeting a sort of stranger, and just experiencing uninhibited mind blowing sex, raw hunger to sex...

The next one was with a partner who taught/allowed me to have multiple orgasms... learnt how to breathe through and take control of the rhythm and slow down, not stop straight after...

F   *Losing my virginity, discovering the joys of oral sex & Fernando. I was lucky - I lost my virginity to a man I loved and who loved me. We were both virgins, so we took ages building up to it. It didn't last long and I didn't come, but that didn't matter. It brought us closer together as a couple, and we could learn what we liked together. The first time I received oral sex was awful - felt like an epileptic slug down there. It took a much older, more experienced man to show me how it was done properly. Fernando was the best 2 night stand I ever had. Again, I was really young and inexperienced, and he was much older with more experience. The thought of him still keeps me warm on those long, cold winter nights!*

G   Hmm...Being beaten and fucked in my wedding dress (and not by my husband)...being totally filled by inflatable dildoes... double penetrated. They are dildos that have a pump attached, with a valve that can be released to deflate quickly. They are made for purpose so won't burst, which would be the main danger. Obviously, you could stretch someone so much that skin tore, but that's where trust comes in. It doesn't do internal damage, nor leave you permanently flabby! Being choked to blackout as I came, there is a risk. Choking is maybe a misnomer, it isn't air being blocked off, its pressure cutting off the blood supply, and you black out very quickly. I always feel like I've been out for ages, but it's only a few seconds. I come round thinking I have been asleep and dreaming, and often panic a bit that my partner will be angry that I fell asleep while playing. When I realise what has happened I laugh like a lunatic.

5   Have you ever wanted, or had, sex with a woman?

A   I have only kissed and allowed a woman to go down on me and I did on her once and found it did nothing for me so never ventured there again, women don't do it for me.

B   *Noooo, never.*

C   I've never had sex with a woman but would love to give it a try.

D   *It's on my to do list with my partners consent. I do get turned on by women, but it's a tenderness thing. I would like to caress some breasts in the way I like to be touched. Does that make sense?*

E   Sex with a woman - Never, but have been asked to, on several occasions, intrigued, but don't think it will ever happen now. Never met the right one in the right circumstances.

F   *Nope.*

G   Curious...never done it and am very picky.

6   Have you ever had a man, you were with, want sex with another man?

A   I have been with a man that has given to a man but never taken. At first it wasn't unpleasant, I suppose a turn on, but that seems to have waned slightly but it doesn't faze me if any man wants to go there. My man doesn't care; a hole is a hole to put it bluntly. I guess that is where we differ. I suppose that is why I cannot love him like I AM supposed to. He doesn't make me feel special in his life.

B   *No I haven't, but I would love to watch my lover being given oral by another guy and even having sex with another man but not another woman.*

C   No.

D   *One boyfriend was very camp, I did wonder about him, but we finished for other reasons. My present partner has been with a man. It doesn't bother me, it was in his youth when he was trying all sorts. He spent a year in Amsterdam and learnt a lot about sex!*

E   No.

F   *No - but he did want to try a threesome with me & a black guy. I have no idea why - it didn't happen.*

G   Not to my knowledge.

7   Would you go to, or have you been to a sex club?

A   Yes. I have been more than once and I would go again if the club is good. The one we went to a few times changed so not that good any more. I would recommend it if the person likes that sort of thing. I wouldn't say it helps the relationship I have it just helps me in respect that I can still feel attractive even though I am not so young, but I guess it may do with other people but cannot speak for those.

B   *Never been, but maybe with the right man I would. I have been tempted a few times.*

C   No.

D   *Have been to "Bizarre Bizzare" in London. I was walked through London tube wearing a collar and lead!! It's not a sex club as such more an event for freaks and uniques, but they had a dungeon for naughty subs. Very sexy night out, saw some of the best boobs ever!!*

E   No, been asked to but never done it.

F   *Nope*

G   Define sex club! Never been to a swingers club, and sex doesn't generally happen at fet clubs. Beatings and needleplay mainly. I have never seen sex happen and hardly ever any overtly sexual activity.

8   Do you like to cuddle, talk and be treated tenderly after sex?

A   Yes I think that is where men are lacking. Cuddling is the most fulfilling end to the evening.

B   *I like a cuddle and to fall asleep on the guys chest. To talk is good as well.*

C   Depends where and when. If you have shagged on the living room floor then lying here having a chat isn't really an option. If you have made love in bed then a cuddle and chat is lovely. Only, of course, if the bloke stays awake!

D   *Yes, but it rarely happens. As long as we are collapsed from an amazing orgasm - being sweaty and sated beats a hug in my book!*

E   Sometimes, for a woman, after orgasm, it can be emotional, I've even cried when you feel it's been love making and not just sex....

F   *Yes, but not for too long. Probably no more than half an hour. Depends on how well I know the guy. If it's a one night stand we're talking 5 minutes, if I have strong feelings, we can go to half an hour, give or take.*

G   Yes. Because what we do is rough, the snuggle time afterwards is very important (aftercare). A "good girl" comment makes me glow.

9 Have you ever had a threesome? Two men, one girl or two girls, one man? Or more?

A   Yes. With men. Once only with a woman not much fun for me. Yes, I have been gang banged and it was right for the time. Again it's what you want at the given moment and the place has to be right and,of course, the men but I have been in many situations where there's been more than 3 people and again can be fun but the right moment. Bukakke is not my cup of tea. I have had some good experiences with groups, but more have been a let down and it tends to put you off a bit. I think it's got to be a good planned party and men that are not sleazy helps. I have had some men that are very nice and seem to care how they play, that is good, that can be a turn on. Some have been turn ons and some not. I don't think sex is a phase; I think it's more who you are with and whether you are in that perfect relationship. Why do people do swinging? I believe it's because although they are fairly happy in their relationship they are not fulfilled sexually. I know if I was in that perfect relationship sex is the most wonderful experience and way of showing someone how to become one (as a couple). Sex is what you make of it and if we say it's a phase it's just telling us we are not happy.

B   *Yes . 2 men.*

C   No

D   *Yes - me with 2 guys. It showed me how powerful my body and mind were, how I could deal with the sensory over load that was happening and how different parts of my body reacted to multiple stimulation - for instance, just after the first time we met up I had my nipples pierced as I felt my breasts and more so my nipples weren't responsive enough. When we met again, I discovered that having responsive nipples was a very good thing and it led to more pleasure for the 3 of us. The friend had always been uncertain of giving oral sex - so we helped him with that. It wasn't crazy and frantic, it was controlled and sexy, safe words were in place and I had a contract with my dom. I would always have a secondary security plan in place and my dom respected this at all times.*

E   No, but again it has been talked about and come close, even explored to find the 'right' one (woman) But never happened....
F   *Nope*
G   Nope. I'd be interested to try. I would love to be double dommed.

10 What is your view on anal sex?
A   Depends on mood and size haha. It can be quite nice, but the size makes a difference. Too big is a no no. Mood also comes into play. Very rarely do I go there, but I have done and would maybe again on occasions.
B   *Yes, I love it.*
C   I would love to give it a go. If both parties want to try it, why not?
D   *If done politely then I love it - don't accept none of this 'oops wrong hole' stuff. For me anal sex can give a more powerful orgasm for both - for me it's the very sensitive girlie bit being sorted, for him it's a different angle and tightness - a change of sensations is great for orgasm! Double penetration, yes, with 2 men and man + toys. This is something the three of us wanted to try and we did with various levels of success - I found it uncomfortable, we didn't get our positioning right and the friend was a bit too eager at times - however, when it was just me and my dom, we used a vibrator, I have enjoyed having the vibrator in either way - however the most mind blowing was riding him (me on top with a butt plug in - I will never forget that orgasm - poor chap nearly drowned!)*
E   It's up to the individuals.
F   *If it's done properly (plenty of warm-up and gently) can be amazing. If not done properly it's agonizing. Not done properly is men being stupid. It's a completely different sensation and makes my clit really sensitive - which is goooood.*
G   Love it. *blush* The harder and deeper the better. Lube is for wimps. I never disliked it. Recently I have found I love it and cum and squirt just from anal. I am such a slut.

11 Do you have any fantasy unfulfilled?
A   Lol yeah, Bruce Willis my final fantasy but luckily I get most of mine fulfilled
B   *Yes. My fantasy is for my guy to be having a poker game and I am the hostess for the evening. At the end of the evening me and my man have sex on the floor with all his friends watching. Then they start to play with*

themselves as they watch me and my guy having sex naked on the floor then all 7 guys cum all over me.

C   Yes, I have unfulfilled fantasies which relate to anal sex and sex with women.

D   Yes - a few in fact.

E   Don't really have any fantasies now. I personally feel for many women a fantasy stays in the mind, maybe never to be fulfilled...

F   I'd have a threesome with 2 guys.

G   Being made to service a succession of men. Of being controlled so much that I will debase myself in that way for his pleasure/amusement. I probably won't do it while I am with my partner because beneath his casual attitude, he is very possessive of me. But he sometimes talks about it when we are fucking because he knows it will make me cum immediately.

12 What makes bad sex?

A   When you are not in the mood and the man still expects it and they don't care if you are not interested or up for it

B   A guy who can't get hard. Doesn't like oral on him. A guy who asks is it in hahah or was that good?A guy who only likes the missionary position. A guy who doesn't make you cum. A guy who pokes his tongue in your vagina and thinks he's doing a good job or licks you like a lollipop haha, boring. A guy who can't do two things at once. Having sex on the same night every week doing the same things.

C   When you don't want it but give in for an easy life and end up faking an orgasm.

D   Define bad sex? I think things that disgust others – it's a taste thing. I now make sure I am fulfilled - I have had lots of bad sex, but I have grown so much sexually in ten years it's a bit hard to answer!

E   Bad sex... errrmmm.... Someone that is selfish... Dirty...!!??

F   A guy that rushes and is only interested in his pleasure.

G   A race to orgasm. No foreplay. Being asked what I want.

13 Have you ever wished you hadn't bothered?

A   Yes. I still sometimes think that on occasions.

B   God yes, every Saturday night with my ex

C   Sometimes I wish I hadn't bothered as in the question about bad sex. Having sex for the sake of it is horrible.

D   Yes - in a bid to get someone else off my mind I seduced a guy off the internet - bad decision! One day I was angry and lonely so I answered an ad online and within six hours I had him! He didn't know what had hit him and I wasn't satisfied so I paid for his taxi home. I was needy for sex - I should have just gone DIY!!

E   Yes !!

F   Yup. Sadly.

G   Far too often.

14 Can you have too much sex?

A   Depends who you are with and, I suppose, your age. The older I am becoming the less I guess I need it and it can sometimes become like a chore but like I say depends on who you are with and how you feel about them.

B   No.

C   Depends on the relationship. When I was seeing the bloke who was 10 years older it was all we did. It was never going to last; sex was all that kept us together. If you are in a long term relationship I don't think you can have too much, if both of you are happy with it.

D   Again depends on what you class as too much. I have friends that have sex only a few times a year!

E   Too much sex... Noooooo!! Well unless one gets too sore... haha. That's happening now for me...lol Ooops, too much info!!

F   I don't know....can you?

G   No!

15 Is kissing important?

A   Yes and it needs to be sensual kissing.

B   Yes, very. Sometimes more passionate than sex itself.

C   Kissing is so important, so why don't I like kissing my husband?!

D   Not to me, as a sub you are rarely kissed with passion. For me giving my body for pleasure doesn't mean I need to be kissed

E   Kissing is very important, pecks on the lips, long deep passionate kissing.... love it.....

F   Oh yes.

G   Kind of. Don't want to spend hours snogging, but a kiss is very erotic...bitten lips also. And to be teased with lips close and then pulled away as I go to kiss...

16 Have you ever had an affair?
A   No, only consensual. I would never cheat.
B   *No, I was single, but the married guy was cheating.*
C   I have and would have another one.
D   *Yes - with a neighbour; it was what ended my marriage. I will say however, that it was due to my husband's neglect in the bedroom department, that was part of the reason for it. In my opinion, or in my case anyway, affairs are because there is something lacking in the relationship. I know I would have an affair again if I wasn't satisfied at home.*
E   I never had an affair whilst I was married, but came close, but managed to keep it 'real' and say "No".. Unlike my ex-husband, who I know had 4 affairs, one lasting 3 years!!!!!
F   *Yes. I'm ashamed to admit it, but I was a bit of a slut in my 20's. I slept around and didn't discriminate much. I always practiced safe sex though. I guess my friends couldn't get their heads around sex outside of a relationship. I was heartbroken and desperate for affection. Only as I got older did I realise I was never gonna get that sleeping around.*
G   An affair as in a regular partner that I cheated with? No. Been unfaithful often though, which is why I believe in poly.
(Authors note: 'poly' as in polygamy – to have more than one regular sexual partner).

17 Are you a fan of porn or don't like it at all?
A   No doesn't interest me in the slightest. More of a man thing I think.
B   *Not really, but if I do I like to watch 2 guys.*
C   I like porn. It can really help a tired sex life.
D   *I enjoy watching porn with my partner, it doesn't do much for me alone, and I have no problem in him watching it alone every now and then, if it became regular thing I would be concerned and ask questions. Porn is a side dish to me being the main course!!*
E   If porn is a shared pleasure between two adults then yes, it can enhance the sexual experience.
E   *I can take it or leave it.*

G   Love it. Although most is badly made. Obviously bdsm, but it has to seem real, like a real couple. I don't like it too glossy and staged. I like to be able to imagine it is me/us. Porn has given us lots of inspiration.

18 Did you read 50 Shades and if so did it do anything for you?

A   No, had no interest in reading it.

B   *Yes I did, it was rubbish. Not raunchy at all. Didn't bother reading books 2 and 3 and its sooooo annoying now that all guys want to be dominant and want the woman to be submissive. Most haven't even read it. Because she actually turns the tables and dominates him. Why can't men/women be equal in the bedroom?*

C   No.

D   *50 Shades was a bit light for me, but I read the trilogy in a weekend. Sylvia Day has written the Crossfire trilogy which for me did a lot more - to the point of masturbation. However a real turn on for me was Indigo Bloome -Destined to - trilogy that hit the mark for me – every woman should read them !*

E   Not read it... yet..

F   *Nope.*

G   Yes I read it. Hated it. Badly written and so annoying that the BDSM is explained by childhood abuse. I discovered it online in about 1997 and it explained a lot about my sexuality. I never could do the "now twiddle my left nipple" kind of stuff that Cosmo advises us to do, I would freeze up. Being told what to do, or just made to do it always worked best for me. The pain stuff was an extension of that.

19 Would you say you are wild and crazy or reserved, compared to your friendship group?

A   I am quite reserved to start with depending on the man or group but can get quite sensual but crazy isn't me . SENSUAL. Kissing, caressing. More making love than just sex. Being able to look in their eyes and give them a loving look to turn them on. Licking them around the inner thigh, whispering nice things in their ear like "What turns you on?"and "How do you like it?" whether rough or soft etc.

B   *Wild and crazy.*

C   I think I come across as reserved, however, most of my friends are too. I have a wild and crazy side that is dying to come out in the bedroom.

D   I'm very reserved unless in the correct situation then I can be wild and naughty or down right dirty!

E   I can be wild and crazy... (something takes/comes over me...!!)

F   I've probably had more partners and had more fun al fresco than they have. I'm not into S&M, bondage etc.

G   Off the scale

20 What are the most adventurous places you've had sex?

A   Middle of a field in daylight is probably the most adventurous and sex clubs in front of people and the back of a mini which was funny. I am not so much a watcher, I don't like watching porn, really doesn't do much for me (as I said earlier), but I like to watch men perform with me so mirrors above can be fun lol.

B   In the toilet of a train . York - Edinburgh twice, the same guy. Also gave a stranger a wank on a train in seat next to me with people sat opposite (behind his newspaper). Sex in a public country park. Sex in a public toilet in a pub.

C   In a cornfield on a very hot day in July. I got sunburnt boobs, I was really young.

D   In a fishing boat, naked off Falmouth Harbour. I'm a nudist too so that has been fun, in the woods, - on a pool table of a pub with a party in the next room. Nothing too raunchy I guess!!

E   At night, at the top of a children's slide in a playground on a holiday park. Out in day light, laid on soft warm grass in an opening within the woods. In a field under the moonlight over the bonnet of a car... By a lake in the snow. On the beach as the tide came in and nearly cut us off...!! Ooops.

F   On a yacht, on a beach, on a hotel balcony overlooking the beach, in a field (I'm a country girl!), boardroom table.

G   Under a tree in the park at the back of my Dad's house

21 Have you ever been caught having sex?

A   Nope

B   Yes, as a teenager. We were parked up down a country lane on a cattle grill, the guys naked arse up at the windscreen and my vibrator on the dash board when the farmer knocked on the window and told us to move on hahaha.

C   Yes. I was 16 and was caught by my parents in my bedroom with my older boyfriend. My dad hit me.

D   *No, I'm far too smart - to the outside world I am sweetness and light, to those that know - I can be all sorts of things. I have been described as 'dangerous' by many men !*

E   No, come close though....

F   *No. Thank God. Although it came pretty close when I was living at my parents'.*

G   Yes, when I was 18, by my boyfriend's younger sister.

22 Have you, or would you ever, pay for sex?

A   I have been paid, but would never pay. Got paid a few times by a man that was not someone that appealed to me, but he would pay us for our company and to please him. Did I care? Not really, he was a slime ball haha, but most men I have met have made me feel special and that is enough for me. It was me and my man, it was someone he knew and the man we used to see loved having my man, the man was a taker and not a giver which pleased my fella. All the man did for me was oral sex so it was ok.

B   *No*

C   No

D   *No I haven't paid for sex - but I would if needed.*

E   Never...

F   *No.*

G   Never have. May do, when I am older and can't get it other ways.

23 What is your view on prostitution?

A   I believe that brothels that are run correctly to be ok, I don't have a problem with this, but think it should be taken off the streets away from children.

B   *I think it should be regulated and legal. Get away from the seedy dirty street walkers and have properly run establishments where the girls/guys are tested for STI's. Issued with condoms and the safety of the girls/guys is guaranteed.*

C   I have no problem with prostitution and think it should all be legal.

D   *To be honest, it's the oldest profession in the world - just very bad marketing. I would have sex for money if it was legal.*

E   When the prostitutes are not forced into it and a guy wants to use one and all clean etc.. Then I feel it's ok - Needs must etc... and whatever turns you on... I would never do it though...

F   *Brothels should be legalised and properly regulated.*

G   It offers a service, and if it were less taboo it would be safer for both sides of the transaction. At my most skint, I seriously considered it. I did private paid photo shoots instead, which came close. I didn't like it. It felt sleazy. Some creep with a camera and no real way of knowing what he would do with the pictures. Him knowing that I was desperate for the cash. I'd do it again properly now though. The reason I didn't do any escorting is because I was scared it would be dangerous and I didn't know how to go about starting.

24   Do you ever wonder if there is someone out there for you that you could spend the rest of your life with or do you have that person?

A   I believe that somewhere out there is that special someone for me that would make myself complete, but, no, I have never met him yet.

B   *I live in hope.....*

C   I have been with my husband for more than 30 years; who wants to admit they made a mistake after all that time?

D   *Ah very interesting, at this moment in time I would say I have all I need. However, as I have hinted upon, my partner and I have relationship rules which have grown over time; if the rules start to be disrespected... I have a sex back up plan should this happen. Sex as you can tell is very important to me.*

E   Wow..! Big question.... I would hope, for all of us, that there is someone... at the moment I'm 6 months into a new relationship with someone I've known for over 34 years..... It's great, we're taking the time to learn all about each other and he's lovely... Hope he's 'The One'!!

F   *Yes. I had an affair with him for most of my 20's,but he was married and wouldn't leave his family. He started off as my friend and we would have lunch together. Everyone at work thought we were having an affair long before we were, so we'd ham it up and come back with glasses and clothing skew whiff when we'd done nothing more racy than have a coffee & a panini. When we did have an affair, no-one took any notice. We were soul mates. We both still miss each other desperately at times.*

G   Not sure I believe in forever, people and circumstances change. But I am with the man who I have most believed could be forever

25 What are your top three romantic films?

A   I loved 'Ghost' for its romantic scenes. 'Dirty Dancing' was good the way the dancing came into play. 'Pretty Woman' and showing how love can come from all walks of life. 'Officer and a Gentleman' was good also. I guess Patrick Swayze and Richard Gere know how to act sensually haha, but Bruce Willis can do it for me in Die Hard haha.

B   *Pretty Woman. Love Actually. Notting Hill*

C   Brokeback Mountain, Brief Encounter, The Notebook

D   *Not got any particular favourites - not really a chick flick girl - although when the '50 Shades' film happens, I will be first in line for tickets!*

E   Romantic films = 'PS I Love You' and 'Notting Hill' - My 3rd was a programme that should be a film...lol. It was called 'Reckless'. Back in the 90's. Brilliant...

F   *'The Holiday', 'Labyrinth' (watch the end bit - David Bowie begging Sarah to love him and let him own her. Sexy, powerful stuff.) & 'My Big Fat Greek Wedding'.*

G   'Gone With the Wind' (where he leaves her at the end!)...'My Fair Lady' (where she realises he's a wanker)...can't think of a 3rd that I like. Oh oh oh...'SECRETARY'!

26   Have I missed any important points?

A   Yes music, it is the best thing to set the mood. Playing the right songs can most certainly help

B   *You could ask if a woman likes to be romanced and foreplay before sex or as a person gets older does sex become less important and friendship more important or does size matter? Does a woman like to get dressed up for sex slutty or classy? Also what turns a woman on ?*

C   What about women faking orgasms? Also women's views on how men view contraception. I think men still see it as a woman's responsibility and that can lead to some very unpleasant and heart-breaking results.

D   *A few of my thoughts are lights on or off? Positions? Set times for sex or spontaneous? Can you talk freely with friends about sex?*

E   Toys - my favs are to do with sensory and movement restriction - spreader bars and ropes, cuffs and clamps, I'm not sure how far to go with this bit !!

F   *Probably. I'll have a think.*

G   I didn't have a clue why people raved about sex until a few years ago. It was ok, pleasant enough, but nothing amazing. Now I know what is possible, thank god. I had been conditioned to think that anything kinky was wrong, I missed out on so much. And why does nobody talk about female ejaculation? I would say that it is amazing and awful. It feels different to the other kind of orgasm. It is messy and I wish I could control when I do and don't because it limits spontaneity. I always have the lingering worry that actually I have pissed myself.

I began this section with a short interview. I will bring it to an end with a longer one; this is from a lady who has done soft porn and lots of modelling shoots. Her view on sex is no less shocking than some of the ladies in the survey, although some of her experiences might be considered extreme by some people.

"Have you ever had a 3sum with you and another girl?

Yes a couple....

Did it do much for you? Was that with your husband?

Lol.Nooooo chance. He's too boring. I loved turning the man on....more than the actual act with girl. I liked watching too.

Watching comes up quite a bit. What do you get out of it?

I just find it horny. I love watching porn too, then jumping in all turned on.

Another common theme. People who like porn definitely seem to like group sex. Would you agree?

Yeah I reckon so. The more the merrier, trust me.

What is the most you've had? In one sitting as it were?

Haha....8, terrible I know!

8 blokes?

Yup lol.

How did that happen? A party? Did you set it up? It must have got very messy.

Hahahaha, yes a party. No, it just happened I was a bit mad, but it was goood.......I get mega wet so can cope.

At a house party that became an orgy?

Yeah, a very naughty party.

Was it just you that got fucked like that or did other women get involved?

Just me.

And did others watch? How do 8 guys fuck you? One starts and his mates join in?

Yeah people did. Messing with a couple of guys sucking them off, then it just got bigger. Bit of dp (double penetration) lol. Lots of sucking, riding, a lot of doggy. Cum on my tits, my face, in my mouth.

I didn't know you liked anal. Do you like dp'ing? It sounds a spectacle to watch.

I love it lol, done right it is lush. Pussy first then add the anal,very good.

So, other than your 8 man gangbang what other group sex have you had?

Oooh lordy...3sums... a few occasions mainly with booze involved.

Is it something you'd do again?

Never say never.

I'm sure you told me you once had 5 guys? Have I remembered right?

(Names a well-known porn star and some recognisable actors) and a couple of randoms. Afterparty sex.

Did you find that more exciting? To be fucked by people who had a 'name'?

Felt naughtier definitely.

Would you say the wildest sex is when you are not emotionally attached, but the best sex is with a person you love?

I dunno. I just like good sex lol....but seem to enjoy missionary more when I'm in love.

You nearly went to a sex club. You haven't been to one before have you?

I did. It was a few years ago, with a mate of (names an actor) in London it was called the F club I think. More because he was hot. Lol. He liked other guys touching me whilst he fucked me. I sucked a few people off, but not much more than that.

Did you find that the size of your boobs made you popular? Is that always the attraction with blokes? Or do you think that blokes just like to fuck a wiling girl? Would you go to a sex club now?

I guess so, probably in that environment they help, but a lot like that I'm so loud and wet. I would if things changed with my current circumstances. I would probably get into that more.

Really? So group sex is definitely your thing then?

Yeah it's hot. I think more because it satisfies me.

How close did you get to going into porn or would you in the future?

I get asked all the time, but that's a bit different because it would be in the public domain etc. I don't think anyone does porn for the sex.

And I hear the money isn't that great either. How do you feel about your experiences with women? Did they do it for you or was it just something that happened?

It depends what you do. Women, for me, was more about turning the guy on; it doesn't really float my boat.

What do you mean, depends what you do? What female experiences did you have then?

In porn if you do more kinky stuff you get paid more. Straight sex is about £500 for 3 scenes. I've shot photo scenes with women and done things with guys and girls when I was younger.

A lot of people that I have spoken to have gone with girls because they wanted to know what it felt like with a girl and for more of the touching, foreplay etc. It wasn't like that for you then?

No, not at all. I'm very touchy feely with my girlfriends, but nothing gets me in that department

So what do you really like?

Hot sex. Hard cock haha, multiple orgasms. However that comes.

Haha. Those times when you had 5 and 8 guys. Did it turn you on being cum on and in by so many guys or was there a point where you thought "Christ, no that's enough"?

No, I loved it all. I'm a bit of a cumslut.

Haha. At the end of all of this do you still like the love side of sex? Being held, kissed, desired or are you a "fuck me hard" sort of girl. I spoke to one lady who said if her fella tried to cuddle her after sex she'd slap him.

Haha, that's funny. I do like cuddles and kisses, see there is still romance in me, despite all my naughtiness."

This is sex in 2015 and it illustrates what people are doing. Some men may be shocked, but a lot of what you have read was hetero-sexual sex, so it's men engaging in this activity as well. It's really important to remember that all of the women who took part in this survey would appear to be 'average' by the casual observer and that's sort of the point. We never know what other people get up to behind closed doors and yet we seem to have a fascination with sex, as if we might be missing out on something. I think it would be fair to say that many people do feel they are missing out and that is all part of communication and engagement with your partner. Knowing what they like, what turns them on, what they don't like and the same is true for you as well. If you don't like something your partner does to you then you have to tell them, getting defensive or irritated is poor quality communication and it will cause problems in the relationship.

Key points to remember:

1   **All the women in the survey were 'average' to the outside world looking in.**

2   **Everyone has their idea of 'normal'.**

3   **There is no such thing as 'normal'**

4   **Great sex comes from excellent communication, spoken and non-verbal.**

5   **You have to have confidence to ask for what you want, but you also have to communicate well to get it.**

6   **Sensitivity is very important to women and many feel that they don't get it from their male partner.**

7   **Sex can help a relationship or kill it, but it is still only one area of importance.**

Chapter 7
Time to start understanding the issue

I hope you found that enlightening; the fact is that even if you think you're strange, odd, weird, or not the same as others, somewhere there will be someone who is indulging in the only really good phrase from '50 Shades' – kinky fuckery. That is, doing something that some people think is 'kinky'; so much of what we regard as 'kinky' is influenced by our upbringing and so much of that depends on when you were brought up.

When I was at school, in the 1960's and 1970's, sex was seen as the great unknown. I lived in London until 1971, having been born in 1963 and not long before I left my primary school we six year olds were shown a film about sex education. I can't remember it now, but I do know that the same film was going to be shown when I moved to Northamptonshire. The parents were asked if they objected to this and enough did that the film wasn't shown. I can't remember if it wasn't shown at all or until I was older, but the fact was the school in London thought small children were old enough to be exposed to a certain amount of 'where the babies come from' education.

Sex education didn't raise its head again until I was around the age of 13 or 14 and then teachers had to endure the educational films of the time. Pornography was a rarity although 'girlie mags' were in abundance. My step-dad always had a stash of them (thanks Dad) and they fascinated me. Paul Raymond was king and *Fiesta*, *Club International*, later *Razzle* as well as *Mayfair* and *Penthouse* were required reading, *Playboy* wasn't so much in evidence – probably too many words in it. Of course I loved the girls, but I also loved the stories and I learnt a great deal from reading them, although misreading a word can be most confusing. I wondered for a fair while why women had 'public' hair. I got there in the end. When I was old enough (shopkeepers asked less questions then) I began buying my own magazines and my fascination with the female form and breasts in particular began at this time. Although I had also had a crush on our 16 year old babysitter (Suzy) at the age of six. Women have long intrigued me.

Access to pornography was a struggle for many years in the pre-internet days. Videos were expensive and so were scan mags; there was even a time when genitals were blocked out by a large red dot. It was a strange time. My proper introduction into pornography was via a couple of *Private* magazines (Scandanavia's finest) with close up cum shots, anal sex and double penetration seen for the first time. In this world of instant access this must seem very strange indeed.

The essence of this book is about seduction and that process was learnt a long time before my interest in magazines and videos, although at the time I had no idea that I was learning it. My father left the family when I was two and a half and my sister was six months old. He was having an affair whilst my mother was carrying my sister and they parted not long after the birth. For a long time I despised him, but in my late twenties realised that I shared certain traits with him, namely a love of women, and boxing, although the two were not connected. What happened as a result of my parents' separation was that I became the sounding board for my mother. I know she had boyfriends at this time (it was a few years before she met my step-dad) – I remember some of the men who came to visit, but what I remember most was my mum talking to me. About what I have no idea, but I would sit and listen and contribute nothing back I imagine, but the process of listening was born and it has stood me in very good stead ever since.

A woman wants a man who will listen to her, to hear what she says and not butt in offering a solution. My earlier recommendation of the books of Allan and Barbara Pease holds even truer now. This couple have done massive amounts of research into the male and female species and I have found all of it to be true, at certain times. I devoured their books, videos and cassette tapes. At the same time I also learnt NLP, I went to the seminars of Tony Robbins and spend two and half years learning Nonviolent Communication from Dr Marshall Rosenberg and his disciples. What I learned will help you immeasurably, from wherever you are attacking this issue.

First, men and women are completely different and to understand them is futile and yet necessary. As Becky Adams once said to me "For a man to understand a woman is like me trying to understand my pug. My pug loves chasing squirrels; I don't know why he does, I certainly don't have any interest in them, but pug loves them. I don't have to know why he does I just have to accept that he does. And so it is with men and women." This is the same Becky Adams who ran brothels for 20 years and had more access to men's sexual proclivities than anyone I have known.

There is also the James Morrison song *You give me something* and the lines "And I can say I've never bought you flowers, I can't work out what they mean", it isn't your job to work out what they mean, just buy her bloody flowers. Boys and girls like different things, sure we all know that by now. Of course people are different and to try and get people to like the thing we like is sometimes difficult and confusing, but the fact is on the whole, women like flowers, chocolates and jewellery. It doesn't mean you should buy it for them when you have cocked up, it works even better when you have done something right.

The biggest problem men have with communication is that they use direct speech and women use indirect. What does that mean?

Men speak in facts and data, whereas women talk about emotions. There is cross over in all of this but these are the trends. One of the things that makes me unusual amongst men is that I can speak about and write about emotions; this gives me an advantage when it comes to talking to women. That doesn't mean I want to talk about shoes, clothes and flowers, but it does mean that I understand a woman who is upset about something. I also know when to shut up and let her talk. It is not my job to find a solution for her, it is my job to listen and give the right amount of nodding, 'yes' and 'no' to her issue. It takes a lot of practice because sometimes the answer is obvious to a man, but a woman often doesn't want to upset someone. An example of this could be that your wife/partner is having a problem with a girl at work. Here's how the conversation might go:

"Hey honey, how was your day?" you ask the appropriate question.

"Not great," she has a face that would freeze grapes.

"Oh no, what happened?" you at this point realise that you have opened not a can of worms, but one of hissing snakes.

"That cow Sally Miller," (if you are Sally Miller I picked your name at random and apologise now), "the bloody problems she caused me today. We have this project going on that I have to make sure that all the documents have to be collated properly. Anyway, I thought I had everything right, but just as I was about to hand the folder to Sally – who has to hand it onto Margaret – I realised that there was a document that was missing. I knew where it was and I could have got it in five minutes and all would have been fine. I told Sally that and she said 'Well, you should have checked before you gave it to me, shouldn't you? I'm not going to give the file to Margaret and have her think that I'm no good at my job. You can tell her'.

I didn't get mad, I said "I understand Sally, yes it was my fault, but if you can give me a couple of minutes I'll get the document and only you and I will know what happened. I'm sorry, but can you wait, just a couple of minutes? Please?" I even smiled at the bitch and do you know what she said?

"No darling, what did she say?" you interject; it is vital to be sincere at this point.

"She said, 'No I bloody can't. The meeting starts at 10am and if I'm late then that's another way I'm going to look like an idiot. You'll have to bloody sort it.'

"I felt awful, but went off to get the document, went back to the meeting a couple of minutes late and told Margaret I'd made a mistake and gave her the document. I felt absolutely terrible." Your wife looks as if she is about to cry at this point.

This whole scenario is fraught with danger and you have to be very wise. To begin with you will want to give her answers to her problem. You will be thinking this way:

"I can understand your problem; of course we all make mistakes and the easiest thing to do would have been to have told Margaret right from the start and derailed that bitch Sally."

This would be a huge mistake, or you might be tempted to try a different approach.

"What you should have said was 'Calm down Sally for Christ's sake. Don't have a heart attack, give me two minutes and we'll get it sorted."

Both of these responses make perfect sense to a man, but a woman doesn't care, certainly not at first. What she wants is for you to shut up and listen to her problems, let her speak and get her emotions lined up. Your thoughts are irrelevant, what she wants from you is support and understanding, which brings us to the next challenge.

Women, on the whole, use 20,000 words or expressions per day. Men use 5,000 words or expressions per day. I'm very much the exception to this rule, but it is a good general rule of thumb. A man will use most of these words and expressions throughout the normal working day and what most men want to do when they get home is the 21st Century version of fire gazing, the pastime developed by our prehistoric ancestors. This might be watching *Top Gear* or *Man vs Food* or playing on an Xbox, reading or sitting in the shed. He has used most of his quota of words and expressions and to cope with 10,000 words coming at him all in one go is tough for the poor guy. If your wife has been at home all day looking after the kids and hasn't spoken to an adult then it becomes even tougher for the husband because she's only used 5,000 words and gestures all day, she has 15,000 left and he is getting all of them whether he likes it or not. This is where conflict occurs. His wife has her problem with Sally and Margaret and she is blurting all this information at him. He's just heard the Wednesday mosh on Radio 2 and now his wife is unloading like a machine gun. His head can't take it and to shut her up he offers her the male answer – they are logical, to the point and should stop all the words.

Unfortunately that isn't what happens at all, what happens is that he offers the sort of support he thinks she needs and she turns on him like a cobra on a mongoose. She might respond with something along the lines of

"Did you listen to a bloody word I said? Do you want to get me fired? I sometimes wonder if you have the brains you were born with."

He now feels hurt, rejected and under-appreciated and she is pissed off with his attitude.

This scenario is repeated night after night across the country and the world – and it never needs to be this way. What has to happen is a clever man will ask his wife when he gets home would she like him to listen like a man or a woman?
If she says a woman he will listen and only offer encouraging sounds of support until she has finished. If she would now like some ideas he will offer them to her; if all she wants to do is vent then she will have vented and they can get on with their evening. Assuming he doesn't have too much to say about his day. If he does, it's now her turn.

The key here is that communication brings you together, lack of communication pulls you apart. The Neil Diamond-Barbra Streisand song *"You don't bring me flowers"* has the line "You hardly talk to me anymore when I come through the door at the end of the day," sums up many couples or the level of conversation is so banal that there is no development in them as a couple or their interest in each other as they grow older. If you've been together for five years or more then you will have changed, but if it's more than ten years then the difference will be immeasurable and the key to staying together is to take note of those changes.

When I started this journey of understanding people more I was lucky to be introduced to Nonviolent Communication, a system devised by a man called Dr Marshall Rosenberg, a Jewish psychiatrist from Detroit. What I learnt from him would transform the way I communicated; it took me a while to understand his method but once I did it was truly revolutionary.

I came across him quite by accident listening to Radio 5 Live one day on the drive into work. It was one of those '*Sliding Door*' moments. A very clever rom-com with added twist – the concept being that if you were delayed by 5 seconds how would your life change?

It's a similar theme explored in the "*Inches*" speech by Al Pacino in the film '*Any Given Sunday*'. One step to the left and you miss the pass, one step to the right and you're a hero. I paraphrase, but that's the principle and so it is in '*Sliding Doors*'. Five seconds early and nothing happens, five seconds late and your life will change, so it was with me listening to Radio 5 Live that day.

Rosenberg was talking to the presenter and asked him "Who is making your life less than wonderful?" I loved that as a question and I still do. There is an immediate presupposition that your life is wonderful and someone is making it less so; it is so much more elegant than asking "Who is pissing you off at the moment?"

The presenter went on to say that he was having difficulties with his partner at the time; it wasn't a major issue, but one of those things that starts small and escalates. The 'leaving the top off of the toothpaste', or 'leaving your shoes in the hallway'-type things.

What impressed me so much about Rosenberg was his calm manner. He never got emotionally involved but worked out the issue from the perspective of feelings and needs. This blew me away and took a while to understand as well.

The idea is this. Needs remain constant, there are only a few of them, whilst feelings change by the second; also the idea that whilst there are only six human needs there are hundreds of different types of feelings.

How quickly can we move from excitement to disappointment, from calm to aroused, from fearful to excited? Even as you have sat there reading this you will have gone through different emotions, but what does it all mean? Why do needs remain constant? I found this so hard to understand as the NVC (Nonviolent Communication) model seemed overly complicated.

Fortunately going to different seminars helped me understand. Tony Robbins is one of the best speakers I've ever seen; he has sold more personal development products than anyone in the world and his seminars are 12,000 people sell outs. He's the guy with the big teeth, the big smile who gets Oprah Winfrey fire walking and appeared in the film *Shallow Hal*; he's the guy who convinces Jack Black, in the movie, to see all women as beautiful. At his 'Unleash the Power Within' seminar he also talked about needs, except he is clear, there are six. Rosenberg often talked about nine, but being the simple person I am six works for me.

The six are certainty, uncertainty, significance, connection, growth and contribution.

Number one: Certainty – without it we will feel anxious – the feeling created by the need not being met. With it we will feel secure – again the feeling created by the need being met. Certainty comes from behaviour as well as circumstance; let me first explain it in simple terms. Wherever you are reading this – in bed, on a chair, on a train etc – you didn't examine the place you are now seated. If it's in a park you definitely didn't, the seat/ground seemed solid and you sat down. Wherever your car is parked you left it in a place you felt was safe. Where you live, I hope, you feel safe there. The way your house is laid out is in a way that you feel secure and all of this gives you certainty.

It's the same with behaviour. If you do something that makes you feel good you are more likely to keep doing it and that is true for bad habits as well as good. People who smoke get satisfaction from it. The same is true of people who take drugs, who drink too much, who can be addicted from anything from sugar to sex. The behaviour gives them certainty. Why do we stay with a particular person? Sometimes long after the love has gone, the phrase "Better the devil you know" is often repeated at this point. Certainty is the starting point of our needs because without it we feel off kilter, not quite right, in short uncertain.

Number two: Uncertainty – and this is where Mother Nature plays her cruel trick. The problem with too much certainty is that human beings get bored very quickly. If you have a job in a factory or a warehouse, and I have worked in both, the work is often laborious and mind numbing, it is very easy to become bored and you work only for the money. This money we then spend on things to make us feel happier about our lives because we hate working just for the money; the irony is not lost here.

It can be the same in a relationship; you begin as most couples do in the throes of passion and can't wait to see each other. The sex is amazing, but how quickly do we become bored with the same positions, the same body, the same touch? Human beings are the oddest of creatures, we desire something for so long and yet allow ourselves to slip into boredom once we have it.

The nature of boredom is simple – a lack of engagement; not being into the subject with enough depth and this is the secret to a great relationship, the depth of communication. We have then two opposing forces, certainty and uncertainty, also known as variety, which everyone knows is the spice of life.

Number three: Significance – we all want to feel that we are important, as so many teenagers will inform us, they just want 'respect', but that is earned, not given by right, although status seems to give that. Perhaps that's why people are so keen to become movie stars or pop icons.

Every year the talent shows like *Britain's Got Talent*, *X Factor* or *The Voice* are full of people wanting to be the next big thing. Some know that they are only there for their five minutes of fame, or notoriety, but many want to be the next Robbie Williams or Adele. The chances of that happening are tiny, but still someone will think 'If they can do it, so can I'. I thought the same whilst writing this book, the only way to write a book, or create anything, is to believe that the world will like it. Not all the world, but the people you reach out to.

Relationships are no different – we all want to be someone else's significant other and when we know that we no longer are it breaks our heart. With all relationships it is important that we begin with ourselves, if we don't think we are important why would anyone else? It's the same with a business – if you don't sound like you believe in it why would anyone spend their money with you?

Number four: Connection/love – isn't this what this book is all about? Connection is love, because without one there isn't the other. It starts at the mind or maybe it starts before, at the eyes. The eyes tell you where the truth is and if you doubt it at all then you can test this with a kiss. In my lonely days I kissed a girl one day, someone who meant a lot to me and it inspired this blog. If you want to understand connection then this sums it up to me: It's called "The touch of a kiss".

I have always considered a kiss to be the most intimate of acts. Not the peck you receive from your mum, or the slobbery, sometimes whiskery lip touch from Grandma or even the slightly food filled kiss of a small child, no, I'm talking about the act of intimacy that passes between two people who like, or love, each other. When kissing stops in a relationship, as far as I'm concerned, it's over. When you see someone who makes you take a sharp intake of breath the next thing you often think is 'what would it be like to kiss them?' If you no longer wonder that why would you want to be with them? Kissing equals attraction, passion, desire, affection, lust, hope and promise. Without that you only have friendship and comfort.

Some people may disagree, but from the number of clients I've seen who express sorrow, anger, depression or frustration with their partner in every case the passion has gone and the kissing went with it. Consider this for a moment. Remember a time when you wanted to kiss someone. Do you remember the fear you had that you may have got the timing wrong or you'd misinterpreted the signals? What happens if they slap me or it all ends in embarrassment? These questions race through our minds as we move closer to the person waiting to feel the soft, slightly wet feeling of their mouth on yours. And then we decide it's time. It is a moment of pure romance, or lust. It is always a moment of passion. You can feel it. Chemicals race through your brain, your breathing speeds up, your skin colour changes and blood is pushed around your body. You know where it goes. You feel alive!

Have you ever felt a kiss days after it had dried in the wind and time had taken away the moment? Where you could feel the pressure of their lips on yours? Perhaps a song brought the feelings back of how good you felt. Or a smell or circumstance. Where you could see the person's face and feel them in your arms. An embrace normally accompanies or follows a great kiss.

This is not about what happens after. Where, in the classier films of the time, the door closes and we don't see what goes on next. This is all about kissing. Of the great kisses of your life where love/lust - take your pick - takes you on a journey unique to the two of you. Where the moon was brighter, the air crisper, the smell of perfume sweeter or the air that surrounded you was like a force field holding you both in. Encapsulated in a physical act of attraction, belief and hope.

Kissing is the extreme act of giving. It's about trust, about offering yourself up, about the future and it begins with a single kiss. From that moment on your life changes.

For some people it means marriage, for some children, for others pain and hurt, for some it is a mistake, for many it is a gift. It's a kiss and yet it's your whole life, your past, present and future. If you have someone in your life, kiss them with real meaning and you won't have to use words to explain how you feel. If you want someone and you think they want you kiss them and you'll know for sure.

For those who are adrift and looking to be kissed reference the great movie kisses: Trevor Howard and Celia Johnson in 'Brief Encounter', Clark Gable and Vivien Leigh in 'Gone With The Wind' or Leonardo di Caprio and Kate Winslett in 'Titanic'. We remember passion and we want to be reminded of it.

Now conquer lips that are yours to kiss or those you want to be yours, waste not another moment of your time in doubt and fill your life with love and kiss that person every day."

Of course connection is more than just the person that we love. It can be the gesture of thanks to a motorist who lets us through or the lack of connection when we are ignored! It can be the casual conversation in a supermarket queue as you wait for the woman with the coupons to count them out.

Facebook has built itself entirely on the socialness of social media; Facebook grew massively when it allowed photos to be posted on the site, suddenly everyone could connect on a deeper level with someone they could see or were tagged with. It is about bringing us closer together.

These are the four main needs, if these are being fulfilled you can move onto the last two.

Number five: Contribution – Obviously it means to give, but give how? There are many ways: anyone who loves to teach, to pass on knowledge is a contributor. The person who wants a friend or someone they know to grow because of something they have learnt or done; that can be anything from simple trivia to a life lesson. Some people interpret contribution as giving to charity, which it can be. I'm sure many of you have particular causes you like to give money to, even if it's only buying a copy of the 'Big Issue' from a street vendor, but others take it to a much higher level. There are some people, like Chuck Feeney (an American who pretty much invented duty free shopping) who gave away $7.6 billion, that's some serious contribution.

The summer of 2014 was filled with a phenomenon known as the Ice Bucket Challenge. It had hung around as a cool idea to raise money for Motor Neurone Disease (ALS or Lou Gehrig's Disease in the USA) for about 18 months and then suddenly it reached the tipping point. Whether that was Mark Zuckerberg challenging Bill Gates to do it or however it happened it was celebrity culture that drove the number of people doing it. Facebook was awash with almost everyone doing it and getting ever more inventive too.

From Charlie Sheen giving away $10,000 to Tom Cruise getting hit with about a dozen buckets of water and even ex-President George Bush Jr doing it. For many it was about the act, but for just as many it was about the act of giving, of contributing to a lesser known charity and feeling good about it. It was contributing on a global scale.

Number six: Growth – the final need of the six. We all need to feel like we are growing and becoming better people in some way, that may be better parents, to grow intellectually, to improve your body, your living circumstances, there are so many ways to better yourself in some way.

Often one of the ways we ignore is to grow as a couple and this is where the problems lie. If one person feels themselves moving away from the identity of the couple they will begin to resent the husband or wife. Whilst as a therapist I saw this many times; in my experience it was usually the wife that felt this way. Many men were happy to be 'together', some content just to have the family at home even though they never did anything. This leads me nicely onto the way of using NVC in a practical way.

Having understood that there are only six human needs, but that many emotions flow from these (feelings) it is now imperative to understand how this works in conjunction with the question "Who is making your life less than wonderful?" The really scary part is that often it is you, but you don't know it until you investigate your feelings of dissatisfaction.

Let's start with a married woman, in her mid-30s, she married in her late teens/early twenties and has realised for a couple of years that her life is slipping away from her. Sometimes she looks in the mirror and she thinks that her looks are fading, or it might be the amount of weight she has put on. Sometimes she has these thoughts in the middle of sex on a Friday or Saturday night (the weekly ritual) as he pumps away unconvincingly whilst she thinks about firemen or Navy officers to stop herself from going dry, but at the same time wonders if she has enough potatoes for dinner tomorrow.

It could be the same conversations she's had with him about fishing or work or money or the kids. Or perhaps it's the way he never puts his shoes away no matter how many times she tells him. To the outside world they are the ideal couple, they have a summer barbecue, they are at parents evenings together, he has a decent job, she works part time walking dogs, the kids are lovely too, but inside her head she knows it's all coming to an end.

What she has is too much certainty; too much of knowing what the sex will be like, what they will be doing on July 15th, where she will be this time next week. She craves excitement – the stereotypical 'bored housewife' syndrome, which is true even if she has a job. It is at times like this that the player finds his prey.

Whilst I was writing this one married man (on learning of the book's title) said "It's easy to seduce someone else's wife, it's seducing your own that is the difficult part." I have to be honest, he is missing the point completely. The happily married woman cannot be seduced, she loves her man and everything about him and that happens when the six human needs are fulfilled. To get back to the challenge.

What does she do? She has too much certainty i.e. she is bored, so what can she do?

To leave him seems an awful mess, in fact she may still love him, but she has realised he is boring and has turned into his dad at the age of 35. A calamity.

This leaves her with a number of options: one, stay with him and endure a life of boredom. Two, have an affair and see if that livens things up. Three, start sleeping with women. Four, suggest new sexual practices that they have never indulged in before. This could start with bondage and toys and could go as far as swinging or dogging. Five, suggest to him that she is bored and they need to do things to stimulate her, outside of sex or six, go back to the original plan and leave him. (These concepts are explored in much greater depth in the following chapters).

All of this takes courage and courage is the one emotion that most people lack. They lack the courage to express themselves and fear rejection or they lack courage to bring up the problem in the first place. Inevitably this leads to a parting of the ways, because they ignore the issue so long it becomes insurmountable. It is usually at this point that people used to seek me out.

Almost every client I ever saw, to do with relationships, was female, however, many of the clients who saw me after the split were male. In today's world 50% to 75% of all marriages will fail (depending on which statistics you read) and in those splits 85% will be initiated by women. In other words, most men never see it coming.

You could say this is down to ignoring the problem, but the simple fact is most of them don't realise anything is wrong. As far as they are concerned the little woman at home is happy, they have enough money and all is well.

This can all be traced back to communication – that thing that women do so well and most men are usually terrible at.

All the way through this book you will hear the same thing being repeated: keep talking, keep communicating and be aware of each other's needs. For some men this is going to be very difficult; they never learnt the art of communication and they think it's too late to start now. Of course, that's just ridiculous. A lot of men will chat for hours in the right environment, whether that's at the pub, the gym or on the golf course. They will talk about all sorts of subjects: women, politics, sport, world poverty, the latest films, what they are reading, trivia, their problems, their health, you name it men will talk about it, so why do they struggle to talk to women so much? Partly because the things women talk about doesn't interest men; things like shoes, fashion, flowers, home furnishings, shopping and the children, which is why some women love gay men so much.

Many gay men have the best of both worlds in this respect. They have the male and female side of the coin, in terms of conversation. All you have to do though, is remember the early days. The looks across the table, the conversations that went on for hours, the talking you did after sex, the cuddles you had and if you are saying, "But that was so long ago," or "But you can't keep that going forever," then the probability that your woman could leave you has just increased. You're giving up before you get started.

If there is one thing I have learnt by writing and researching this book it is this, the amount of diversity out there is enormous, but it still comes back to the same things: connection, listening, giving and wanting the fairy tale to continue.

Herein also lies a problem; there are those who have been hurt a number of times and don't believe the fairy tale does exist. They believe that they were lied to by Disney and all of his happy ending cartoons, but I do believe in it. I've been hurt, I've been lied to, I've hurt others and lied to them, but I still believe in love. I still believe in romance and I will never stop believing in it because I have far more wonderful experiences than painful ones. The fact is that when I have been totally honest the quality of my relationship is so much better.

Isn't that the problem with too many relationships? We start by putting on a show, we dress our best and we act our best, which is good, but when our partner discovers our failings it can come as a terrible shock.

When you start from a point of honesty it removes that disappointment and allows you to freely express yourself. To not be judged, to be accepted and willing to grow as an individual and as a couple. That is the key; you don't have to like all the same things, but it is important you do things together and have enough in common to start with to build a life together.

The biggest mistake that people make is to take their partner for granted; to believe that they will never leave. This is particularly true for the man who controls his woman through subtle psychological control either through intimidation or guilt, but it also true of all of us.

When I was in my twenties I fell in love for the first time; I was 23 and she was 18. She was small, curvy, pretty and we were mad about each other; for a while all was well. We moved in together and people talked about us in couple terms, we were seen as a dream couple. We moved into a flat which had a basement bedroom which we thought was great; that was until the winter came when everything became damp. Sleeping in it wasn't pleasant – I had a full set of Belstaffs which went green with mould. The whole environment affected our relationship and she decided to move back to her parents although we continued to see each other. This was after a couple of years; after a while we decided that we liked living together but not in that flat and we got another flat about a mile away, which was huge and on the second floor so no more damp problems.

In those days I was an angry young man and would lose my temper and act like a child, we would row and generally be silly. Getting older has benefits and as I said NVC got rid of most of my anger issues, but in my twenties I wasn't always the sharpest tool in the box. I also used to spend a lot of time doing the things I wanted to do (in my case it was martial arts training, running and weights – you could replace those with any male pastime) and she used to say to me "You love training more than you love me."

As a young man I would reply "Of course I don't, it's just different." What I wasn't doing was giving her enough significance and connection, but we bumbled along. We even got engaged and had a party. It was at this party that we were given two carriage clocks (it was the done thing in the eighties) and flippantly I said "Oh, that's good, if we split up we can have one each." She wasn't impressed. I just thought she had a poor sense of humour, I'm sure she thought I was an idiot.

We never got to the wedding though. I knew things weren't right; I can remember being at her mum's house one Sunday afternoon and I was invited to go away with them for a few days in Wales and I turned it down. Something in my life was more important; it wasn't but in my naivety I thought we would be together forever. I loved her, but didn't tell her enough, didn't show her enough and one day I plucked up the courage to ask her, as she clearly wasn't happy, if she still loved me. It was a May Bank Holiday Monday and she was lying on the sofa. She looked at me and found the courage to reply "No." It was the worst rejection I had ever received and yet, in hindsight, it was completely obvious. On the Saturday, six days later, she left me and my heart broke into a thousand pieces. I didn't truly get over her until I fell in love again a few years later. I learnt a valuable lesson though, when you feel something is wrong it definitely is wrong.

As soon as you get that feeling you should act, it might still be too late, but you have to give yourself a fighting chance. Far too many people do what I did and assume that because you've been together for x number of years that it will always be that way. Remember, in relationships that end 85% of the people who leave are the women. That means you screwed up and didn't do enough to save the relationship. It's no good trying to feed the horse in the barn when it's already running in the meadow. I was right though; we did both end up with a carriage clock.

What all of this means is that you have work to do. This book is primarily aimed at men in the full knowledge that it will be mostly read by women; what does that mean? It means that men don't spend enough time learning how to be better communicators which means that they will never really understand their women and that's why they will find themselves, at some point, on their own. And they will blame everyone else for their problems except themselves.

In the movie *Crazy, Stupid Love*, Steve Carrell is left by his wife (she has an affair) and each night he goes to a bar and tells everyone what has happened to him. It only stops when the character played by Ryan Gosling tells him to stop whining and get with the programme. In his words he tells Carrell he has to find out who he is all over again. It is the curse of many people in relationships, they cease to be individuals and become this intertwined entity that in so many cases comes to a horrible end.

As a therapist the great majority of my clients were in the 30-50 age range. They would come to see me for sleep problems, relationship issues, anxiety, depression, the fear that they were slip, sliding away, to heighten self-esteem and to have phobias cured. They would also come to have addictions to food, drugs and cigarettes ended. Why this age range in particular?

I think a number of reasons; one, that they have been with someone a long time and they are bored; two, that they have enough money to sort the issues; three, that they feel over-whelmed and don't know what to do about it; four, they lack the courage to make a significant change in their life.

When people look at their future most will ask the question "But what if it all goes wrong?" A much better question would be "What if it all went right?" The first question causes fear, the second creates excitement. Far too many spend time running away from the things they don't want and not enough time rushing towards the things they do want.

If the main point of this chapter has been about communication we need to spend time on understanding the area of a relationship that most women crave and most men fail at: romance, the subject of our the next chapter.

Key points to remember:

1   **Do we have to learn how to understand each other?**
2   **Direct speech vs indirect speech**
3   **How a man should listen to a woman, which is probably not the way he does now.**
4   **5,000 words vs 20,000 words**
5   **The 6 human needs:**
       (a) Certainty
       (b) Uncertainty
       (c) Significance
       (d) Connection/Love
       (e) Contribution
       (f) Growth
6   **Keep talking to each other**
7   **Honesty**

Chapter 8
They want to be loved

Doesn't everyone? Isn't that the point of the book? To find someone to fall in love with you and for you to love someone else back, even with the person you fell in love years ago and forgot how you did it.

As discussed much earlier men and women are such different creatures, the things that turn us on are different, the things that liven us up are as well. Straight men rarely get excited by shoes or handbags. We find *Mamma Mia* interminable and don't find *Bridesmaids* funny either; in turn straight women tend to have no interest in *Escape to Victory* or most things football related.

We talk about different things and talk in different ways, so how does the miracle of relationship happen at all? Because at brief points we find common ground and the way to find more common ground is by using the concept of romance.

I do accept that this isn't true for some people, but for the majority romance is where the magic happens. The sex may be amazing, the conversation sparkling after and the laughs may flow with great gusto but romance is what sets the pulses rising, makes the serotonin flow, dumps the dopamine into the blood stream and sets everything racing. What do you do if you are not naturally romantic? At this point you become ever more pleased that you bought this book. Romance 101 begins.

Let's start with the easy stuff. What you think, as a man, is not important; this is about keeping your lady happy. If this was a business book, and lots of the principles are true of business, this chapter would be about getting inside the head of your customer. Instead this is about listening and learning; men are notoriously hopeless at this. They have a problem with their filters; they are set to facts and data when women are talking emotion.

Listen to a woman describe shoes: "I have to have them." "They are gorgeous." Those shoes would make me so happy." "Where did you get your shoes from honey? I would die for them." Straight men have no clue why shoes elicit such emotions from women, but here's the good news, you don't have to know or worry, just accept that they do. This is very important so I'll repeat it, men speak in facts and data and women speak about emotions. Remember this and you will go a very long way.

The same is true of handbags and clothes; her wardrobe may be full but she has nothing to wear. Your job is not to point out that her wardrobe is full, your job is to either go shopping with her or if you are really smart agree to meet in a mutual meeting spot 2-3 hours later. This way you can trawl the places you want to go and she gets to spend money. If you do get taken along then be interested, even if you'd rather be anywhere else! All of this is major point scoring in the great points table that she keeps in her head.

Yes, she really does this. Every woman has a different method of calculation, but they all do it. You cutting the grass is one point. Washing the car – one point. Fixing the toilet seat – one point. All that physical stuff that you think is doing you good is way down the scale compared to emotional connection. Telling her she looks lovely – 5 points. Not saying she is lovely minus 10 points. It's unfair but it's her game. Listening to her when she comes in after a hard day – 10 points. Giving her solutions after 20 minutes, minus 15 points. Just listen, dummy. Remember she will ask for your advice when she wants it. And so this goes on, your woman wants emotional fulfilment and if you don't give it to her you will miss out.

Hopefully you are getting the message now, listening is the key to getting a woman to fall in love with you. With the listening under control what do you talk about? Everything and anything.

Find out what she is interested in and if you don't know much about it, or don't know anything about it, don't try and wing it. Nothing is worse than showing you are a twat when you try to avoid being one. If you try and wing it she'll know. Try and understand her interest; people are interested in so many things. It could be dance music, history, places to visit, learn her dreams and as you come closer together, make plans to do stuff together.

One relationship I was in we talked about going to Portmerion in Wales. If you don't know where it is, it is on the Welsh coast not that far from Snowdonia. It's where the 60s cult series *The Prisoner* was filmed. The appeal of the place goes far beyond *The Prisoner* though, it is quirky, pretty and unique.

My girlfriend and I talked about going there for 10 years and never went together. She went on her own not long after we split up and I've been a couple of times now. It takes four hours to get there from where I live. Four bloody hours and we talked about it for so long. When you have a passion (or your partner does) to go somewhere, go there. Experience it together because when you found out she's been with someone else you are going to be gutted.

Romance is about sharing; that might be watching a movie sitting on the sofa, but hopefully you will have deeper dreams as well. Imagine that place you've always wanted to go and standing looking out to sea, holding hands and wondering what you will do with your future. It can also be a nightmare. Some years ago I sat on a beach with someone I didn't want to be with wishing someone else was there. Fulfil your dreams with the person who makes your world light up. Share your dreams, plan your life and let that person into your heart. If you've been hurt before that isn't always easy, but the only way to feel love again is to let them in. Even if they don't say it at first you will see it in their eyes.

I am a lover of stories; that is whether I read them, hear them or experience them through the medium of television, the cinema or a DVD and what I want to share with you now are the films that I believe every man who wants to understand romance should watch. For some people you will think that this isn't your thing; that doesn't matter. Remember, you are trying to get inside her brain and affect emotions.

These movies each give a different clue to romance, love and the thoughts that affect a woman's mind. It doesn't hurt that every one of these films is a good movie on its own merits. Some are classics, most have humour in them and some are inspiring. I have chosen these to help you understand the process of romance. They will also give you lots to talk about when you first meet, or when you are trying to rekindle a broken romance. Romance leads to passion and passion leads to love. Each film will have a brief breakdown of the synopsis, with no plot spoilers and a lesson that you can take away from it.

I would ask you not to make the mistake of thinking this isn't relevant to you. This isn't just about movies; it is about the stories and lessons I learnt from each film which will, hopefully, resonate with you. The Bible is a book full of teaching tales; it doesn't matter whether you believe in God or not a lot of the time, it is still about stories that teach lessons. Stories like the Good Samaritan, Noah and the Ark, Moses and the parting of the Red Sea. You know all of these because they were drummed into you at school and these films serve a similar purpose. To educate, amuse, inspire and teach you how to seduce your wife – and to continue the theme, anyone else's!

The first on the list is *The Notebook* – Ryan Gosling, Rachel McAdams, James Garner and Gena Rowlands. Directed by Nick Cassavetes and based on the book by Nicholas Sparks. This is one of those rare movies where the film is better than the book. It is also lovely because it is based on a true story, about Nicholas Sparks wife's grandparents and how they came to be together. They also stayed together for many years, although the twists and turns in the story are not revealed by that fact.

The story is as follows. It begins in a retirement home; an old man reads a story to an old lady suffering from Alzheimer's Disease. She is happy for him to read to her and he describes how Noah and Allie meet each other at a fairground and how Noah has a tough time getting her to go on a date with him. Finally she succumbs and she learns they are from very different backgrounds. He earns 40 cents an hour at the local lumber yard, her father is a millionaire and she is due to go to college (University) at the end of the summer holiday. That doesn't stand in the way of young love though and very soon they are inseparable. One night, not long before she is due to go away they go to a derelict mansion and make love in one of the rooms. Their bliss is disturbed by one of their friends finding them and telling them that Allie's parents have the police looking for them as it is 2am. When they get back to Allie's parent's house a row ensues and Noah storms off claiming that the affair is over. The following day both want to make up but can't find each other. Allie heads off to New York leaving Noah in Georgia.

Noah is determined she won't forget him and writes to her every day for a year, but never receives a reply; the reason for that is that her mother hides the letters. She thinks Noah has forgotten her and he thinks the same of Allie. At this point the Second World War intervenes. Noah fights in Africa and Europe whilst Allie signs up for the Nursing Corps. It is whilst helping soldiers that she meets Lon Hammond, after a short courtship they fall in love and set a date to be married. He is a wealthy man and approved of by her parents.

Meanwhile, the war has ended and Noah has returned home whilst his father has sold the family home and with Noah's G I Bill money they buy the mansion that Noah has always dreamed of owning. It takes him a year to renovate the wreck of a home during which time his father dies. When the mansion is restored to its former glory the local paper takes a photo and runs a story in the news. It is this story that Allie sees almost on the eve of her wedding. She tells Lon that she needs some time to herself and goes to visit Noah, taking him by surprise. The rekindling is passionate and life changing, but is brought to an abrupt halt by the arrival of Allie's mother. During an exchange whereby Allie is given all of Noah's 365 letters, Allie's mother leaves her to decide what her future will be. Throughout this the narrative is told as a story by Duke and the lady with Alzheimer's, so that the whole film is seen in flashbacks. The crux of the film is, of course, who does Allie go to? Her true love, Noah, or marry for money with Lon? That is for you the viewer to learn.

The Notebook could be seen as sentimental trash and by critics it does seem to be viewed that way, but by women (and a great number of men) it is the perfect love story. Young love, separation, love lasting over time (it is seven years from when Noah and Allie are separated to when they see each other again at the mansion) and the spirit of hope and romance that pervades the whole film.

The film keeps the spirit of the book – which is very well written by Nicholas Sparks, but for me the film has a better ending. In Romance 101 this should be the first film on your list to watch. If you are going to watch it with someone then I recommend you save it for someone very special; it's a film which touches the soul and you will want to be with that person when you see it. It will give you both hope and faith in love. If you see it on your own I recommend you don't see it if you are feeling sad, tears will ensue otherwise.

Number two on the list is *Brief Encounter*. Made in 1945 this is the bittersweet romance starring Trevor Howard and Celia Johnson, directed by David Lean. Lean had a habit of making wonderful movies (*Lawrence of Arabia* and *Bridge on the River Kwai* being two of his most famous), but this is amongst his best. Sweet, charming and almost ridiculous at times – those perfect English accents – nothing sums up failed romance better. It is no plot spoiler to tell you what happens in this film, the title gives it away, but it is the perfection with which it is executed which makes the film so brilliant and again should be in your canon of understanding romance. Is it better to have loved and lost than never to have loved at all?

Having experienced all the emotions this film invokes I have to say yes. You wouldn't be reading this book now if not for the past romances I have had. To learn the lessons from the Devil is better than having trod the path yourself, where danger is concerned anyway – and love is a most dangerous path.

Brief Encounter began life as a one act play by Noel Coward called *Still Lives* and was set entirely in the refreshment room of the train station. Throughout the film this refreshment room plays a supporting role, but it was when the play was fleshed out to an 86 minute film that it took on mythical status. Combined with the soundtrack of Rachmaninov's *Piano Concerto No 2* the film tugged at the heart strings and caused a million tears around the world.

The main protagonists (Laura Jesson and Dr Alec Harvey) are both married but meet at the refreshment room of the train station set in the imaginary town of Milford Junction. Laura gets some grit in her eye (the wonder of steam trains) which the good doctor gets out with the aid of a handkerchief. The following week they bump into each other in the town and later again at the local tea rooms. It would appear that fate is pushing them together. How many of us have felt this? They go to the movies together in the afternoon (all quite innocently) and end their day talking back at the refreshment room. Just before their trains arrive Alec asks to see her again. She agrees.

The meetings follow this pattern, a once a week tryst where very little happens and yet you can see these two falling in love and with British sensibility fighting the urge. The idea of the sanctity of marriage stays throughout the film. It is a most chaste of films and more rewarding because of it. There is one scene, in Alec's friends flat, where they almost commit the act of adultery but they are disturbed when the friend comes home early (Alec has a spare key to the flat). This is as close to sex as the film comes; I like this film because of this. In a world of porn one click away this idea of chastity and passion only seen in a kiss is refreshing and quaint, even in a film almost 70 years old.

Like *The Notebook* the film is seen mostly in flashback with Celia Johnson providing the narration and the affair comes to an abrupt end when Alec accepts a job in Africa. The final scene in the refreshment room (where the film begins as well) is so painful when an acquaintance of Laura's bumps into them as they are saying their farewells. You want to give the woman a slap as she chatters on quite unaware of the pain the two are suffering. The final touch when Alec places a firm hand on Laura's shoulder instead of the normal Hollywood embrace and kiss that we are used to seeing is poignant and painful. A brief encounter it most definitely is.

There was a brief run of a stage show based on the film which I saw in Northampton some years ago. It started almost in comedic fashion and the first act was one that you wondered if it was going to work. The second act was a tour de force with great use of the piano concerto. My partner and I came out of the theatre and couldn't speak for around five minutes or so, we were so deeply moved. Upper class, very posh and yet completely wonderful. There has never been a better film about a failed love affair. I can't recommend it enough.

If you fall in love with the film as I have you can experience it even further. Carnforth train station (where the exterior shots were filmed) have a lovely tea room set exactly as it was in the film, although the film set was in Hertfordshire. It's a lovely place to sit with someone you love and imagine Laura and Alec and also hope for more success in your romantic adventures. Carnforth (for your information) is off junction 35 of the M6; if you're ever in the area go to the train station and visit this little slice of romantic history and make some of your own.

Number three is a real adult fairytale: *Pretty Woman*. This was the first film I ever bought without having first seen it at the cinema and I was rewarded in every way. Starring Julia Roberts and Richard Gere, directed by Garry Marshall, this is the perfect modern fairytale, leaving even Cinderella in the wings. Roberts and Gere are never better (and considering *Erin Brockovich* and *Officer and a Gentleman* this is praise indeed), the script is tight, the supporting cast brilliant – particularly Hector Elizondo as the hotel manager, Barney Thompson. The story is that Edward Lewis finds himself in downtown Los Angeles in a Lotus that he can't drive properly and he is lost. He pulls over to the side of the road and asks for directions. The person he asks is street prostitute Vivian Ward (at this point total suspension of belief is asked with Julia Roberts in thigh length boots and a blonde wig), she tells him she will take him to his location for $100 to which he agrees. When they arrive at the hotel which was his destination he asks her to come up to his room with him, producing one of the many laugh out loud moments as she gets into the elevator. An enjoyable night occurs (although much less explicit than might be expected) and the following morning Edward offers her a business proposition. She will be his 'date' for the week for $3000. She accepts gladly.

She also gets a sizeable shopping allowance, but has problems when the shop girls of Beverly Hills are cruel to her. First Barney and later Edward come to her rescue. One of my favourite scenes is the 'sucking up scene'. Money does indeed help shop staff to deliver excellent service and so much fun to make your lady happy if you get the chance to recreate it. Edward's main associate doesn't take quite the same shine to Vivian and when a deal doesn't go his way he blames her for it, trying to sexually assault her to be rescued by Edward. It is at this point that the movie addresses an important point, that of self-esteem.

The film is a complete fantasy, but it does also ask the question of Vivian, how does she see herself? As an equal to Edward (the millionaire business man) or still a street hooker hustling for tricks? By the way she turns down his offer of being a kept woman it shows great self-belief, not something that people in real life always show.

The ending comes when Edward races to her apartment as she is about to leave Los Angeles, thinking their affair over. The final scene on the stairs of the fire escape where they tell each other that they have rescued one another to the sounds of Verdi has entered romantic cinematic history.

There really is no better fairytale. Suspend your belief about prostitution and the likelihood of any of this happening, enjoy the film, the stars performances, a killer soundtrack and the joy that this film invokes. I love it and girls adore it; an important point to remember, about the girls, not me.

Don Juan de Marco is a Johnny Depp movie that many people won't be aware of. Also starring Marlon Brando and Faye Dunaway I've always found it somewhat surprising that more people don't know about it, considering the cast, but what a film. It opens with a scene of the 21 year old Don Juan strolling into a restaurant at a hotel in full Don Juan get up including mask and cape. It is clothing bound to attract attention – amazing how attention grabbing clothing is recommended by those that teach *The Game* i.e. players and in this case it definitely works.

He approaches a lovely lady sitting at a table alone and asks, politely, if he may sit with her. She explains that she is waiting for someone to which he replies, in a Spanish accent, "I will not linger." She allows him to sit.

His patter comes out quickly but elegantly. He explains how a woman's hand is like her legs, her knuckles like her knees and the top of her hand, that base of her fingers…he pauses and kisses between the knuckles. The next scene is of them in bed and she cries out in orgasm as the Mexican band plays in the restaurant below. He returns her to her table just as her suitor arrives, but not so he realises what happens. As Don Juan leaves the restaurant he says "And now I must die."

We next see him atop a billboard threatening to jump and this is when Marlon Brando is introduced as a psychiatrist who talks him down. Depp is taken to a mental hospital and there his tale unfolds. As it does so we are treated to lessons in love and love making, along with a healthy dose of humour and the re-introduction of love into the marriage of the characters of Brando and Dunaway. It is a lovely, warm and funny film, with the Bryan Adams song *Have you ever loved a woman?* as its soundtrack.

It will bring knowledge to your life and a unique experience in romantic movies.

All of these recommendations are used to help you understand all facets of romance, the different ways that writers approach the subject, the way that actors interpret the roles, every relationship is different. Each time you fall in love it is different and you can't fake love either, it happens or it doesn't.

When love collides it is the most beautiful feeling in the world, when it dies it is the most painful, when not returned the most wounding, when lost the most careless.

True love is eternal and never dies, but it doesn't mean it always works. Frank Sinatra and Ava Gardner nearly drove each other mad, as did Richard Burton and Elizabeth Taylor; their love was driven by lust, but unchecked by reason. It burned so bright that it couldn't be sustained. Sometimes turning down the temperature a little is what is needed, just be careful not to let the gas go out. Love takes work and a desire from both of you to make it work.

Which brings us to *The Princess Bride*.

Made in 1987 and not a big hit at the cinema this was a film much like *The Shawshank Redemption* in terms of fan base which grew in popularity on video and later on dvd. Starring Cary Elwes and Robin Wright, with comedy cameos from Billy Crystal and many others it begins as a fairytale read by grandfather Peter Falk to grandson Fred Savage, a big star in *The Wonder Years* at the time.

It tells the story of Westley and Buttercup; her the farmer's daughter, he the farm boy. She would order him around and to her every order he would reply "As you wish." In time she felt herself falling in love with this boy and she also realised that every time he said "As you wish" he was saying "I love you." Their love blossoms but Westley realises he cannot marry her as a lowly farm boy so sets off to seek his fortune where he will return when he is a man of means. She doesn't hear from him for a long time, but does hear that he is captured and killed by the Dread Pirate Roberts.

This concept of separation comes up time and again in romantic films, signifying that love is rarely linear and travels a great many turns before it comes together.

Not long after she learns this Prince Humperdink decides that she will be his bride (herein lies the title) totally against her will. Before the wedding can happen she is kidnapped by Vezzini, Fezzik the Giant and the master swordsman, Inigo Montoya. This results in a chase whereby a mysterious masked man follows them, defeating the three in turn to save Buttercup.

I do realise that all of these names are ridiculous, but the majesty of the film sweeps you along. As it takes you Westley will die and be resurrected (not in a Christ-like way), there is much sword play, the concept of revenge is explored as is torture and comedy. All this in a PG rated movie. I often judge someone on whether they like this film as to whether I want that person in my life. It is not some regular ho hum fairytale as it says in the movie trailer.

To see romance from a man's perspective the place to start is *Jerry Maguire*, made at a time when Tom Cruise wasn't an acquired taste, I still like most of his movies I have to say.

This film by Cameron Crowe begins as a film about sports and sports agents, but with the introduction of Renee Zelwegger it shifts very much into a love story.

It begins with Jerry Maguire having an epiphany about how the sports agents business is and how he wants it to be. He writes all of this down and posts it to each agent at a conference; initial feedback is highly positive, but all of them think he is an idiot and he gets fired from his agency. No one wants less money and care more for the client, is he bloody mad? The agency he works for sacks him and he sets out on his own with his one client, Cuba 'Show me the money' Gooding Jr, and Dorothy Boyd as his PA, the only person who believes in him.

Dorothy and Jerry start dating and this leads to marriage, but it's clear early on that it isn't working. They separate and Jerry follows his errant client across the country watching his star rise. In the later scenes Gooding Jr comes right and they earn a massive contract. Jerry realises he only wants to tell one person this, to share the feeling and he flies back home. When he walks into the house there is a woman's meeting of mainly ex-wives, but Jerry delivers his killer speech where he tells Dorothy that she 'completes him'. Her reply is that "He had her at 'Hello'. Later reprised in the Beyoncé song *Hello*.

It's a film delivered with passion and humour; Dorothy is a single mum and Jerry is willing to take on her young son – a sure sign for most women that he is serious.

I have heard of many occasions where men balk if they find out a woman has children. I have to say I find this distasteful at the least; if you love the woman you take on all the responsibilities and baggage in the hope that you can support and help her through anything. The deal is that she supports you in return.

This is something that is said at the end of *Pretty Woman*. Edward says to Vivian that he has come to rescue her and asks what she will do in return. Her reply is that she will "Rescue him right back." This is what love is about.

The coming together of souls, not just the best sex, not just your hopes and dreams, but the belief that every part of your past, present and future comes together to make your life the best it can be. That waking up with the one is the feeling you want to repeat every day, that looking at her face will make

your heart soar and your spirit rise. That she will help you through the hard times, love you through the good times and be with you for all your days. *The Notebook* praises this, *Jerry Maguire* makes you believe it is possible.

Onwards into the world of fantasy we go now with Francis Ford Coppola's version of *Bram Stoker's Dracula*. With a cast that includes Sir Anthony Hopkins, Gary Oldman and Winona Rider, only Keanu Reeves is a distraction with his completely wooden acting. Oldman is brilliant as Dracula and Ryder innocent and still sexy as Mina.

What sets this movie apart from the Hammer movies of the 50s and 60s is the passion of the sexuality. Obviously the Hammer movies were erotic for their time, not just Christopher Lee, but also Ingrid Pitt and all the beautiful starlets, but Coppola's version and Oldman's acting brings such passion to the character.

My favourite scene happens late in the movie when Dr Van Helsing and his posse are chasing down Dracula and find him with Mina in a bedroom. Just before this, Dracula is struggling with wanting to take Mina as his lover and condemn her to the undead and he is fighting the urge. She looks him in the eyes and says with raw passion "Take me away from all this death."

He cuts his chest and she drinks his blood. The symbolism, the drinking of the blood, the giving of herself, all make the heart soar and you can feel the passion flood through your veins. This is what love is all about, to give yourself whole, without fear of consequence, to drown in ecstasy and know that although only a moment it will live within you forever.

When I did the sex survey I asked ladies' opinions on the most romantic movies and one title came up more than any other, that was *Notting Hill*, another Julia Roberts film, this time co-starring Hugh Grant.

Why it is such a good film? Grant's foppish Englishman serves its purpose well; Roberts is totally believable as the movie star and Rhys Ifans is brilliant as Spike, Grant's flat mate. There are other English actors throughout the film and it does have a feel of a sequel to *Four Weddings and a Funeral* which I don't deem anywhere near good enough to get in my list.

It also follows the theme of love being a meandering path; *Notting Hill* is rarely linear and often goes through many painful times. In this respect I like the sense of twisting and turning before the happy ending arrives, it reflects the way love often is.

The problems of social status are dealt with in a different way in *Notting Hill* with Julia Roberts being the 'rich girl' and Hugh Grant being the 'poor boy', almost like *Pretty Woman* in reverse. Although well-acted and well written (by Richard Curtis) it is the struggle that I think people relate to so much in this film. The comedy moments definitely help, but it is this understanding that love isn't easy that resonates so much in this film, and the unbelievably happy ending of course.

It would seem entirely appropriate to follow up one Richard Curtis film with another and that is *Love Actually*, a total ensemble piece with a number of stories intertwined.

My criticism of this film is that there are too many stories for them all to work well, but as a film it works brilliantly. The child's story particularly grates and the one with the American woman and her brother in the hospital just fizzles out as if even the film loses interest in them.

Colin Firth's story of the writer who escapes and falls in love with the Portugese girl resonates with this particular writer. My favourite scene is the one with Keira Knightley and Andrew Lincoln when he holds up cards proclaiming his love for her when pretending to be a carol singer. Until this point she had thought he didn't like her because he acted so odd when he was around her. A good example that even women can't spot an admirer sometimes.

Men tend to be absolutely useless at this, as a young man I had no idea when a woman fancied me and never picked up anyone in a nightclub when all my peers seem to do so with ease. It wouldn't be until my thirties that I started to see the signs. Women, and their better emotional intelligence, are usually much better at spotting 'fancy me' signals.

Other parts of the movie give us hope that love can be good: the silly stories of Colin going to America and the porn stars falling in love don't really work for me either, but they are fun.

It's the real studies of love with Alan Rickman, his secretary played by Heike Makatsch and his wife, Emma Thompson that stand out. Thompson's performance when she discovers the necklace he bought for Christmas wasn't for her is the stand out of the whole movie, a masterclass in acting and in eliciting the emotions. For a book about affairs and affairs of the heart this is an excellent scene which shows the pain affairs can bring.

As with most of Richard Curtis' films all's well that ends well and we see Martine McCutcheon (who looks gorgeous in this film) getting the Prime Minister, Hugh Grant, as a boyfriend; Colin returns from America a prime stud, Rickman and Thompson are still on very dodgy ground and the closing scenes of real people meeting each other at the Heathrow Arrivals Gate are a great example of seeing real love in people's eyes. That pure joy of seeing someone you love when you haven't seen them for a period of time.

You know you're insane when it is a few days and your heart aches, for some they can cope with months apart. I know I'm not one of them. 'Love Actually' begins and ends at Heathrow Airport because this is where Curtis (as the writer) makes his point, that love is all around. Cue Bill Nighy.

The next film requires some work by the viewer as it in Italian with subtitles, (unless you speak Italian of course), but the reward for the extra work is offset by the quality and experience.

I first became aware of *Life is Beautiful* when I saw Robert Bengini accept his Oscar for best foreign language film at the 1999 Awards ceremony. Walking on the back of the chairs to accept his award with pure joy; the scene played around the world and no doubt helped the number of people who became aware of his film.

He looked totally surprised to win the best actor Oscar as well beating Tom Hanks in *Saving Private Ryan* and Edward Norton in *American History X*, amongst others. Both *Ryan* and *X* are brilliant films so you would have to imagine that *Life is Beautiful* and Benigni's performance are extra-ordinary and in this you would be right. It is one of my top three films of all time and touched me more deeply than most films ever have.

When it begins you have no concept of where this film is going to go. It starts with Bengini as 'Guido' in a runaway car with his friend, the car's brakes have failed. It hurtles downhill eventually crashing onto a farm where he meets a girl who is in a barn. She can't get down and he encourages her to jump where he promises he will catch her, which he does and they both fall into some hay. Immediately he christens her 'Principessa' (princess), although her name is Dora.

Guido has moved to Tuscany and becomes a waiter at a hotel where is enthusiasm wins over many of the clientele including a German businessman. It is during one memorable bicycle ride into town that Guido bumps into Dora again, literally, by knocking her over. He dusts her down, apologises and begins his eccentric way of wooing her. In an entirely appropriate story line for this book he learns that she is to marry someone else and Guido decides this cannot happen. She is, after all his 'principessa'.

The adventures are at the very least bizarre, including a green horse along the way, but Dora realises she is in love with Guido and they marry. In effect this is the first part of the film over; it is almost like a play in this respect.

The second half opens 5 years later and with the nature of anti-semitism affecting the country. In time Guido is taken away by the Nazis and Dora and their little boy also end up in the same death camp. It is at this point that the film changes from being a romantic comedy to something far more sinister, but also the character of Guido deepens as he hides his little boy from the Nazis (they would kill him immediately) whilst his love for Dora burns so brightly.

The genius of the character of Guido is that he pretends all of this is a game so that the little boy doesn't become scared, he tells his son that the winner of the game will receive a tank. It would be pertinent to keep the ending to myself here.

This is a film which shows that love transcends everything; it gives you power and strength beyond which you think you can survive and you still find the will to go on.

In Viktor Frankl's masterpiece of a book *Man's Search for Meaning* he describes how (as a prisoner in Auschwitz) one day he awoke and saw a clear vision of his wife. He was certain she was dead, but had this feeling he would see her as he headed out on a work detail to lay roads. All day he had this feeling that she was near him, but he didn't see her. He never saw her again, but the vision gave him the strength to carry on and he survived to live a full life after the war. He claimed that her love helped him to live, he was sure that the vision was the moment she died and that was what had visited him.

Whether we believe it or not the fact is that it helped him survive a Hell greater than most of us will ever experience. It is here that *Life is Beautiful* makes you believe in love as a power beyond all others.

A change of pace for 2005's controversial love story *Brokeback Mountain*. Directed by Ang Lee whose previous credits include *Hulk* and *Crouching Tiger, Hidden Dragon* this was a film that no one could have expected from him or the stars Heath Ledger as Ennis Del Mar or Jake Gyllenhall as Jack Twist. To see Gyllenhall in *Jarhead* or Ledger as *The Joker* could anything be further from the parts they played here?

When the film first came out it was known by many as 'the gay cowboy movie'; only by those who hadn't seen the film though. Once seen most people were profoundly affected.

When you first see the film it is the suddenness of the love affair that takes you by surprise. It follows the tale of two individuals brought together by the work of tending sheep – one of the ironies of the film is the term 'gay cowboys' when really they are shepherds – on a mountain in Wyoming.

One night they spend a night in a tent together (they have slept separately until then) and pounce on each other. I can remember being surprised as I watched this scene in the cinema, but you accept it as the storyline and carry on watching. What unfolds is a mixture of deep romance, denial, surprise and the experience of watching these two characters struggle with the gay side of their personality.

The film beginning in 1963 sets the tone of the film; unlike the modern day, same sex relationships were not accepted in the 60s in America. It is fear of getting caught and being punished that stops Ennis from committing to Jack.

How many of us have felt that outside circumstances influence our relationships when the truth is that only we can control what we do in our personal lives? You find yourself watching *Brokeback Mountain* wishing that Ennis would find a place for him and Jack to live happily ever after.

With the end of the film you might also conjecture that Ennis must have wished he did. The brutal murder of Jack (for being gay) happens in seconds and is the third major shock in the film, with the first sex scene being the first.

I realise this is a spoiler but it helps to explain the film. When Ennis receives the postcard he has sent returned with the word 'Deceased' printed across it you find yourself gasping and exclaiming "No". Even seeing it a third time still the shock was there. What a way to find out the love of your life has passed away.

When Ennis phones Jack's wife you can hear the unspoken knowledge between Anne Hathaway and Heath Ledger as they talk about Jack and how he knew Jack. When Hathaway expresses her doubt that Brokeback Mountain exists (where Jack wanted his ashes spread) Ledger/Ennis explains that it is very much real. It would seem at this point that Hathaway/Lureen Newsome understands the relationship the two had. The second major shock in the film was when Jack and Ennis see each other for the first time in 4 years. The kiss they give each other is extremely passionate and unrestrained; they hide from the street but not from Ennis' house and when his wife sees them you can feel her sense of betrayal.

It makes you question two things: one, how would you feel if you saw the person you love kissing someone else and two, would that be feeling be worse if you saw them kissing someone of the same sex, especially if you had no idea they were gay?

The final scene when Ennis is holding Jack's shirt and knowing that his life will be without his soulmate is heartbreaking and extremely powerful.

One of the many messages I took from this film is that you shouldn't hang around making excuses; life really is too short. We have no idea when it might end and we have to be true to ourselves and not worry what other people may say.

The 'or anyone else's' part of the book acknowledges that whilst many affairs happen because of sex it would also be true that many people also fall in love as a result of these affairs and that's where the tough decisions happen. Leaving your husband or wife isn't easy but if you're in love with someone else (and not with your husband or wife) then why would you stay with them? There is a great quote that comes up on the internet, attributed to Johnny Depp:

"If you love two people at the same time always choose the second one, because if you'd really been in love with the first you wouldn't have fallen for the second."

And he's right. All affairs start with the attraction and the promise of sex if not sex itself, but when it turns to love it makes life so much more complicated. Hardly anyone ever thinks of the future until their past seems to be all there is to consider.

Finally I come to movie number 12. A film almost mythical in its status, an epic, a true Hollywood blockbuster and one of the greatest romances of the 20th Century.

With Clark Gable playing Rhett Butler and Vivian Leigh playing Scarlett O'Hara this is *Gone with the Wind*. It really is one of the greatest films of all time and so much is right about this film.

I saw it when it was re-issued at the cinema in 1980/81; I saw it on the Tuesday night then went back Wednesday and Friday that week to absorb this amazing film. No matter that it was announced that week that it would be shown that Christmas on television, this film should be seen at the cinema. Epic in scale, epic in length (over 4 hours) and epic in performance, everything hinges on the relationship between Rhett Butler and Scarlet O'Hara and yet most people know that it is a most unsatisfactory ending.

Like lots of these films I re-watched *GWTW*. I wasn't disappointed – for a film made in 1939 its spectacle is amazing, the colours, the scale and the performances are all magical.

At the heart of it are the two main characters, but also the love affairs contained within. Scarlett is obsessed with Ashley Wilkes who is intent on marrying his cousin, Melanie. Rhett is in turn obsessed with Scarlett. Throughout famine and feast this merry go round continues until Rhett and Scarlett finally marry.

As so often happens, tragedy isn't that far around the corner and with the death of their daughter in a riding accident Rhett and Scarlett find themselves without a reason to be together. His famous parting line of "Frankly my dear, I don't give a damn" comes from his utter despair at trying to give Scarlett so much for such a long time and still she seems intent on trying to capture Ashley's heart, particularly true with the death of Melanie. Although Scarlett insists that she does love Rhett and is over her infatuation with Ashley. It is this that Rhett observes and thinks "to hell with it all". Scarlett famously resolves to win back Rhett and rebuild Tara, the plantation home, "After all, tomorrow is another day."

Gone with the Wind is from a bygone era; a world before the horrors of the Second World War (Gable's own wife, Carole Lombard, would be killed in a flying accident during the war), a world coming out of the Depression and a world before rock n roll, the sexual revolution and the trials and tribulations of the late 20th Century.

It is full of colour, of hope, of tragedy, but also of resurrection, whether in the form of the rebuilding of the South after the American Civil War or of the ingenuity of Scarlett O'Hara. She does have a remarkably thick skin.

What lessons are we left with?

First of all, when someone declares their love for you, and you care about them too, stop chasing some half arsed dream of someone who might want to be with you because your ego decries it.

Secondly, don't chase anyone who doesn't want to be with you.

Thirdly, don't be surprised to find yourself dumped if you treat someone badly.

But finally, remember that Scarlett was right all along – that no matter how bad things are tomorrow is always another day. Never give up and always remember the long term; it is short term pain that can cripple you and stop you from making decisions. Perseverance and hope will carry you a very long way.

I wonder how many of these films you will take the time to watch? I wonder if you think there is any point in watching any of them as I have described them all to you?

Some are well known, others not so much, but I have tried to share with you films that will touch your soul in many and varied ways. It is stories that move us, they always have done from *Aesops Fables*, to the stories of the Bible, onward through *Paddington Bear* and *Stig of the Dump*, *Harry Potter*, the novels of Dan Brown and the comedy of Robin Williams, Steve Martin, Michael McIntyre and John Bishop amongst many, a good story will keep us engaged, engrossed and intrigued. So a true love story should as well, particularly if it is your love story.

Too often we forget how to love, as if time and tide pass us by without the simple act of sharing conversation over dinner or a glass of wine. As if we have to go to a restaurant to recapture the love we could have at our own dining table, away from the children, the television or that insidious companion, social media.

The irony that the more social media we have the less social contact we accept and receive. Love is about looking into each other's eyes and seeing emotion; it is about the touch of a passing hand, the replacing of a lock of hair, it is about moments of intimacy which have nothing to do with sex and everything to do with connection.

We have no idea on a daily basis whose head we turn, who looks at us and wishes they could have us.

Facebook has made engagement so easy and yet with the level of love that I am discussing we can reduce it to what it is, a tool for business and a means to an end, to pass videos of cats and Darwin Award contenders.

The secret conversation of the stolen lovers will exist throughout the 1 billion users, but you can sleep peacefully at night knowing that that person you love is not using it to message their lover. That when they go to bed they awake to see your eyes looking at them, that when they are at work they ache to see you again and that where-ever you are they love only you.

This is seduction at its highest, deepest level, the amazing sex is a by-product of the connection that you two have. This is the level you should aspire to and then work to maintain; it takes time, it takes effort and the rewards are what you receive. Not what you deserve, but what you receive.

Key points to remember:

1   **The points system**
2   **The Notebook – even time cannot stop love if it's what you truly feel**

3   **Brief Encounter – better to have loved than never loved at all**

4   **Pretty Woman – love can be found in the most unlikely of places**

5   **Don Juan de Marco – romance is the giving of the soul**

6   **The Princess Bride – it's never over until you give up**

7   **Jerry Maguire – sharing a dream**

8   **Bram Stoker's Dracula – passion is everything**

9   **Notting Hill – distance is no barrier to love**

10   **Love Actually – love is 'everywhere'**

11   **Life Is Beautiful – in the darkest of days, love can give you hope**

12   **Brokeback Mountain – don't let other people keep you apart**

13   **Gone With The Wind – tomorrow is another day**

14   **Keep telling each other your daily stories, it's all about connection**

Chapter 9

And now we begin

I make no bones about it, love is a tricky devil and takes an almighty amount of work to get it right.

Up to now we've talked about the problems a relationship can get into, but also the importance of sex and the passion that it brings to a love affair. I had a client once, a male, who said that everything he did was for his wife; his whole work ethic was for the family and the subject of sex came up. I asked him how often they had sex and he said they hadn't for four years. That was staggering to me and not because I am sex mad, but because it signifies the death of a relationship.

When we first start seeing someone all we think about is getting them naked and having them in every room of the house, in a cinema, a plane, anywhere that brings more excitement and uniqueness to the relationship. In the longest relationship I've had the sex was great from the beginning to the end. We may have drifted as people, but our lust for each other didn't. I'm not saying people don't go through times where they are not up for it, but it is true that without sex and without kissing you are just best friends and best friends isn't enough.

There is a reason that a woman doesn't have sex with you; somehow, in some way, she is upset with you. Anyone who thinks that women want or need sex less than men is crazy, so if she's not having it with you it might be that she's having it with someone else. It could also be that she is ill, of course, or has other things on her mind, but every woman I ever had an affair with told me that they were bored with sex at home and that's why they started looking around.

Equally, although I have talked a lot about women having affairs men do as well, often with someone else who is married. However, whilst doing the research for this book I became grateful for knowing people that are gay; their insight into a world I know nothing about was fascinating. I talked earlier about the use of social media in conducting affairs, but there are also apps on smartphones that make this even easier. I was told about the world of Grindr, an app that you can download for free and it's like an immediate dating site – as in you can find men who want to have sex with another man in the local vicinity. This is the age of technology.

It seems that it isn't only women who aren't getting what they want from sex; for men who are bisexual or gay same sex affairs are also common and leads once more into the world of deceit. Not that being gay is bad, of course, but the essence of this book is to encourage honesty – which must seem a little strange as I've told you that I've had affairs. We'll return to this shortly.

First of all let me remind you of the options I was talking about in chapter 7. These are for the woman who wonders if her marriage is over or if she can save it.

The options were one, stay with him and endure a life of boredom. Two, have an affair and see if that livens things up. Three, start sleeping with women. Four, suggest new sexual practices that they have never indulged in before. This could start with bondage and toys and could go as far as swinging or dogging. Five, suggest to him that she is bored and they need to do things to stimulate her, outside of sex or six, go back to the original plan and leave him.

Option one: stay with him and endure a life of boredom and/or misery. Why would anyone do this in a world full of possibility?

The answer is fear.

When you have been with someone for a long time, that's at least five years, it is easy to forget that there is a world other than you two, it is easy to forget that other people find you attractive and more importantly it is easy to forget that you exist as an individual.

I talked earlier about the insidious form of control that some men have over their partner, building on the idea that no-one else would see anything in you, but it isn't true.

In my treatment room I saw every combination of people you could ever imagine and it convinced me that there is a person (at least one) for every person on the planet.

This was borne out to me when the couple came to see me who suffered from vertigo; there was a host of other ailments, but this was one of them. They had even met at a vertigo sufferers support group; I don't know about you, but my first question (which I never asked them) was "Who goes on top?" Presumably they had managed to get this issue sorted and they did seem to be devoted to each other, but it did confirm that the idea that there is someone for everyone.

I also happen to think that if there is one then there are definitely others too. So what is it that people fear so much? The most obvious pressing question is that they are worried about being on their own. If you're used to sleeping with someone every night (or thereabouts) for five to thirty years a bed on your own can be a frightening prospect. Funnily enough for me it wasn't the sleeping that was the difficult part, for me it was the sound of silence.

When you are used to asking the same person for help, support and guidance for a long time to have that taken away from you is scary. After all, who would you talk to?

The answer, anyone.

You will be amazed how quickly new friends enter your life, whether as partners or as friends. That voice you knew so well may have gone, but advice and friendship are never far away. That's two fears overcome, so why else would you stay where you are? It may be a lack of vision; when Tony told me that more women would want to sleep with me than I could possibly imagine I didn't believe him. I really thought he was being an outrageous friend with a warped sense of humour, but it didn't take long before I discovered it was real.

If you are a woman reading this I can tell you now that if the opportunities were there for me they will be there for you tenfold.

How do I know that?

From the women I spoke to on dating sites; they are inundated. Yes, there are a lot of creeps out there, but there are genuine guys as well. When I was on a dating site I wasn't looking for a one night stand I was looking for a partner; it never worked out that way though. I found my time on dating sites a bit soul destroying really; the people I was meeting weren't right for me, nor I for them.

One memorable evening in London not long before Christmas I had a wonderful date with a lovely lady – we went to Winter Wonderland, rode the big wheel, walked to Leicester Square from Hyde Park, missed the last Tube and had to catch a night bus to get my car for me to give her a lift home. We talked and talked, held hands and were like young lovers; when I dropped her at her house she gave me a kiss and we said we'd arrange another date in the week. A few days later she said she had decided she wanted a baby and a man who lived closer to her home.

When you think you've had a perfect date and still you end up without a foreseeable future it takes its toll.

I got off the dating sites and concentrated on my business which ultimately led to this book; so option one is stay as you are. It does seem like a tough option though. If you also feel like you can't leave him, if you're in an abusive relationship, for example, I deal with that in some depth in a later chapter.

Key points to remember:

1   Sex: heterosexual, gay and bisexual
2   Review of the six options
3   There is someone for everyone
4   Why are you staying when there is so much opportunity outside?

Chapter 10
Is it time to stray?

Option two, have an affair and see if it livens things up.

This book is all about affairs, whether from personal or anecdotal evidence. How many people have had affairs that you know? How many affairs have you had? For a while I wondered if I could ever be loyal to someone else again, but when I look back at my history I was in one relationship for 3 ½ years and another for 11 years and was completely faithful so it isn't that I couldn't be monogamous, it is the degree of love that makes you want to be faithful.

You lose interest in having sex with other people when you are so into someone else; for most people anyway, although I will be exploring a different aspect to that as well. When you don't feel attracted to your partner or they make you feel unloved that's when you are tempted by someone else.

I'm not saying that you don't find other people attractive, that's crazy. Have you ever considered how many people a day think you look good? It's an interesting idea because as I go about my daily business I see many attractive people, so it must make sense that some others might think the same of me. I'm not talking about pure 'look at me' vanity, but when you consider that you might be attractive to someone of the opposite, or same, sex it makes you think about yourself in a positive way. Beauty is in the eye of the beholder indeed.

How can affairs liven up a marriage? First let us assume that the marriage is a good one, except for the sex. I heard this many times "I love him, but the sex is awful." They would then list the different reasons why their husband was a poor lover: premature ejaculation – totally frustrating for the wife. She will forgive him at first "these things happen darling, don't worry", but eventually she will realise that her sex life is never going to last much longer than five minutes. Oh well, at least it will give her time to do all those jobs that need doing! Penile erection dysfunction – he can't get it up. It happens to everyone at some point – yes, even me. It was a bizarre situation.

It was in my wild and exotic days and I had no trouble with anyone else except this one lady; it completely confused me too as she was lovely, elegant and very attractive, but for some reason we weren't connecting. It ended not long after this started happening, quite rightly too, for both of us.

However, this has been my only experience of it and reflecting on it now I understand why it happened. It was the lady's lack of sexual confidence. She was lovely, but didn't make me feel desired, an important lesson for me. Could I have improved the situation with communication? Almost certainly, but at that time in my life I wasn't at my best, another lesson learned.

The condition is usually associated with stress – so much of a man's libido is controlled by his mood and stress is a killer for an erection. Thoughts come to you at the most inappropriate times and then you can't get it back, not a good situation, but imagine if it happens to you in a relationship. There are many cures for this condition and all should be considered because, again, your lady is only going to be supportive (if that's the right word) for so long.

There are a thousand other reasons for a lady to look elsewhere for thrilling sex; it could be that you have managed to land yourself a lousy lover. The idea for this book originally came about because I couldn't believe that men didn't know that the neck is an erogenous zone. How do I know this? Because I was told it happened in conversations and at more intimate times. How do men not know this? Part of this is answered in the sex survey. So many ladies answered about men's sexual prowess by saying they were in too much of a hurry, they don't listen and they are too busy trying to get to an orgasm. It has been said many times by many people but it cannot be stressed enough men are like a gas hob, light the gas and they are ready to go. A woman is like an oven, you have to let her warm up but when she is at the right temperature she can go for hours.

Is it any wonder that women are curious about other women? More on that shortly.

Back to the subject, you have kissed her neck, now pay attention to her back; I know men think all the fun is at the front, but stroke a lady, kiss her back and massage her and she will be yours. Her entire body is an erogenous zone and done properly you can get her turned on by just mentioning what you did last time. If you have never tried sexual hypnosis then you have to give this a try.

Having learnt NLP one day I thought I would try to elicit feelings of lust, it made sense to me that if I could get someone to feel more confident or more excited by using this method it seemed possible that it would with lust. It does. First of all this is a visualisation exercise, so the person on the other end of this needs to keep their eyes shut the whole time. They also need to be relaxed and willing to try something new. To try this for the first time I would get your partner to lie down on a bed or sit on a sofa so she is really comfortable. Start by getting her to close her eyes and think of a time when she was really relaxed; get her to take a deep breathe, hold for a few seconds then exhale. Repeat this twice more. Now use this script. It should be delivered calmly and in measured tones, not loud, not fast, slightly deeper than normal and controlled.

"Whilst you lie there, feeling relaxed, I'd like you to think of a time when you felt really relaxed. It could be on a beach, on a bed, in a chair, but somewhere you felt totally comfortable. Have you found something?"

It is important to establish that they have or you won't have a starting point. We assume they have replied positively.

"I'd like you to visualize that place in your mind, see it clearly, can you do that?"

Now obviously they can, but it is good to check and make sure the image they have is clear. At this point it is also good to see if they see a movie or a still image. What you want, ideally, is a movie; that helps them to see the experience more in real time.

"Do you see it as a movie or a still image? Ok, do you see it small or like a 42inch plasma screen? The bigger you see the image the more you feel the emotions."

When you feel confident they are seeing something nice and you can see them relax, you will see their breathing change and tension leave their body, then you can move onto the sensory experience.

"Where do you feel relaxation first? I know most people don't think about this, but when you become tuned into your body you can feel where feelings start and where they go to in your body, so where do you relax first? Is it your neck or does the tension drain from your head? Some people feel it in their hands first."

You will find that as soon as you mention a particular place most people find that they become aware of the sensations in those body parts, you may have even felt it yourself. Once you have established the start point (let's say it is the shoulders) follow the points as the feeling move.

"From the shoulders does it go up or down? It moves down? Ok, does it move to your arms or your chest? Your arms? Nice. Next your chest or back? Your back?"

At this point you can help to guide the feeling.

"Feel that relaxation going down the muscles in your back and as it moves feel your chest relax and your breathing become a little deeper. Feel that feeling and double it. Don't think about it, it will naturally happen ."

This is true. If you tell the mind to double something it doesn't think about it, it happens all by itself. This is because division and multiplication are subconscious processes whereas addition and subtraction are conscious processes. If you say 'double that feeling' it happens straight away. All of this has to be done without rushing or forcing the process. It must feel natural.

"From your chest feel your hands relax, and move that feeling through the hips, slowly down your legs and then into your feet, feeling all the time your body become more and more relaxed. As you breathe in you will feel the process begin at your shoulders again and as you breathe out you will feel your head relax as well and with each breath you will relax more and more."

By controlling the thoughts at a subconscious level (giving commands that they find acceptable) you are helping the person relax quickly and deeply. It as this point that the process changes. Remember all of this is being done with consent with the outcome being a deeper sexual experience.

"I'd like to take you to another place now. A sexier place. You and I know that you always feel hornier when you are relaxed so now you're feeling good I want you to think of a time, or a number of times, when you felt really turned on. Can you do that?"

You'll notice now that we start to repeat certain elements of the relaxation process. This is because all feelings start in the brain, obviously, and are triggered by words and images. This is why this works so well. It doesn't matter whether the person on the receiving end learns or responds more visually, more with words or with feelings – each cognitive system is exploited and enhanced. When she has found the first or her favourite experience then we can move on.

"When you think of this time do you see it as a movie? Do you see it in colour or black and white?" Colour is more vivid.

"Think about what we did earlier and when you think of this movie think of it on a 60" plasma screen on the wall. See everything clearly. Is that ok?"

Keep checking on her progress. By now she should be feeling more turned on.

"Where do the feelings start? Are they in your head, in your nipples or between your legs?"

Once this is established you do the same process as you did with relaxation, getting them to build those feelings with each cycle. Remember to keep doubling the feelings and take your time with this. The rewards are massive and she will thank you for it as well.

Some of you will doubt that this works, that's fine, whatever works for you, but you must spend time on her. There is always the time and a place for a quickie, but the better you know your lady the easier it is for you to get her turned on.

This book is called 'How to seduce your wife' for a reason, most men forget how to and that's one of the reasons why so many women leave.. Other than her neck, back and getting inside her head you can't forget her hands, behind her ear (only nibble the ear if you are asked to, most women aren't big fans), the inside of her thigh. Some women like their feet being touched, others hate it.

I'm reminded of one of the replies in the sex survey where one guy did something to this lady and when she said she didn't like it his reply was "But my last girlfriend did." This is as sure a way to get kicked out as any.

What is important for women is that they must expect more from their husbands. They may have been raging studs in their teens and twenties, but many men in their thirties, forties and definitely fifties let themselves go – emotionally and physically.

They think they have scored and there is no more to do – this is why the divorce rate is so high; not because there are so many players out there, but because there are so many unhappy women fed up of lazy men.

For those women who indulge in affairs it can keep the marriage alive; not because he knows about it, but because it fulfils her need for good sex whilst the husband fulfils her need for companionship, love, safety and security.

What about the morality? That is down to the individual and how they feel. I have known of many women who haven't felt any guilt and I have known equally as many who are torn up inside by the affair, but still love the sex.

Problems can occur in two ways; the most obvious one being if the parties fall for each other, that will change the dynamic in the marriage and often end to it ending. Alternatively, the lady in question may feel used.

As many ladies explained "He will only contact me if he thinks I'm happy at home, that way he knows there is no emotional involvement and it's just sex."

It's a challenge, because on the one hand she only wants the person for sex (so is she using him or her?), but on the other who wants to feel like they are not wanted beyond the bedroom?

Unless it is a service being paid for, of course.

Affairs can only happen if people are not happy with their regular partner, which brings us to a deeper understanding of the title of the book.

How do you seduce "anyone else's" partner?

The same way you seduced your own.

Communicate, engage, listen and be connected. It's how relationships develop and if you don't pay attention there will always be someone else who will.

Key points to remember:

1   **If you are having poor sex at home would it be ok to have an affair, if it meant keeping the marriage together?**

2   **Men heat up like a gas hob, women are more like an oven. They heat up gradually, but keep their heat for longer.**

3   **Sexual hypnosis.**

4   **Expect a higher standard from each other.**

5   **Morality? It's a personal choice.**

Chapter 11

The softer touch

We move now to option three. What happens when she starts to think about women? Many years ago a good friend of mine came home from a great weekend of sport and being with friends to be confronted by his wife who announced she was leaving him, however the twist was that she was leaving him for a woman. It took him some time to recover from this double blow (that his wife was leaving and for someone of the same sex), but as he looked back he found himself increasingly surprised that he hadn't realised her tendencies before. "She was more of a bloke than I was. At the time I thought it was because we got on so well that she could express an opinion about a girl on the TV or in a magazine." He's philosophical about it these days; it's something that must have happened to many.

When Alfred Kinsey published his volume on women's sexuality in 1953 the wave of public opinion turned against him; the irony was that the book sold in greater quantities than the male volume, but Americans didn't want to be confronted with the truth – namely that women liked sex, they liked a lot of sex and they liked variety. In the Bible bashing belt regions of the USA the thought that women would sleep with other women was abhorrent to them. Poor Kinsey never recovered from this rejection of his life work and he died three years after its publication. It seemed that the biggest problems that the public had was that they realised that all the affairs the men had been claiming to have in the study on male sexuality was true and was backed up by the women in the 1953 report.

There was a rippling of discontent that there were 'homos' out there – male attitudes were the same pretty much up until not that long ago really: "They can do what they want but they had better not come near me." I never understood that, why would a gay man be interested in a beer swilling redneck? However, gay women were a whole other ball game, to steal the pun.

It may have been many males fantasy to watch two lesbians together, but Kinsey's research proved that it was your daughter, your sister, your girlfriend or your wife who was indulging in carnal pleasures of the female kind. Poor America imploded at this news.

Fast forward to the 21st Century and attitudes have definitely relaxed, but from my perspective there does seem to be a lot more bisexuality and lesbians around than the 1970s and 1980s when I was growing up, or perhaps there is just a more open attitude now.

In the 1990s I first became aware of a shift in attitudes, I had dated women who expressed an interest in sleeping with a woman – "Just to know what it was like", but wasn't aware of anyone who had until I became a therapist. There were so many problems that people came to me with that could be traced back to an unhappy relationship and often that was linked to sex too.

When I set out to write this I did wonder whether I had become too wrapped up in the question of the importance of sex in a relationship, but more and more people talked to me about their sex lives. Was that an example of the RAS effect I talked about earlier? Where you become interested in a subject and then you find more people interested in that same subject? I questioned that, but I don't think it is. It could be the that genesis of the idea of this book tied in with the *50 Shades* phenomenon and the increase in the public interest of sex for women and the explosion of 'mummy porn'.

Throughout 2012 the *50 Shades* trilogy became the biggest publishing sensation since *Harry Potter* and in some ways exceeded even J.K. Rowling's success. Worldwide it sold 75 million copies; in one week in June it sold 1.4 million copies and E.L. James (the author) outsold the top 250 authors combined for 16 consecutive weeks at one point. Quite simply it was a phenomenon and no doubt when the first film is released on Valentine's Day 2015 the whole thing will become even bigger.

I wonder how many of you have read it. The briefest of synopsis is that a young girl aged 21 (Anastasia Steele) meets 27 year old Christian Grey, an impossibly rich businessman in Seattle, on the western side of the USA. She interviews him for a local student magazine when her friend is too ill to attend. Anastasia is geeky, awkward and in awe of this man, who takes an immediate shine to Ana and stalks her (in a less than obvious way) to get himself into the position of being her boyfriend. His seduction works, they have a few money orientated fantasy dates (helicopter flights, nice restaurants, beautiful apartment) – it's a cross between *Pretty Woman* and *Indecent Proposal* at this point and then he drops his bombshell. He wants her, but as his submissive; he is a dominant and he has the 'Red Room of Pain'. Here he has taken all his previous conquests, he refuses to call them girlfriends, taking them in all sorts of ways, on crosses, over a four poster bed, on the floor whilst whipping them, subjecting them various erotic tortures and a butt plug. He wants to do the same to Ana, but in order for her to accept him she must sign a contract.

This was the point that most women complained about – all the rest was fine, but a contract where Ana would obey him in every way was seen as a step backward for women's rights. Clearly most people hadn't read Pauline Reage's *Story of O*, a story far more erotic and depraved, if that is the right word. More extreme might be a better way of putting it.

In *50 Shades* Ana agrees to most of Christian's demands and they set off on a journey of debauchery, sex, very expensive presents and the two fall in love. The first book ends when Ana leaves Christian when she doesn't believe she can go far enough to keep him happy. She is also unhappy with the influence of Elena (Mrs Robinson) who introduced Christian to the BDSM lifestyle by her abuse of him. This is the part that the BDSM community really don't like as it takes the stance, in the book, that you must be 'damaged' to be into the practices of BDSM.

Whether or not E.L. James really thought that who knows, but it does seem very judgemental of the practice of domination whilst at the same time being a celebration of it.

If I have already put in a plot spoiler then skip over the next bit as I reveal what happens in books two and three: *50 Shades Deeper* and *50 Shades Freed*.

Book two introduces an element of suspense into the story. Ana and Christian get back together (obviously they can't live without each other) and she learns more about his dodgy past with an explanation of the character of Mrs Robinson and a loopy ex coming into the picture. Ana gets a job, they argue about her working, her boss tries to come onto her. It rattles on for a few hundred pages and then they get married.

Book three describes their honeymoon, a bit more of a thriller with the ex-boss, Ana is a hero, Christian is a bigger hero. She gets pregnant, he goes mad, she gets the hump, all calms down, she gets an Audi R8 for her birthday and it all finishes with them in their 'Grand Designs' home and two children to live happily ever after. I did quite like the thoughts of Christian right at the end of the book, but I have to say that I got through all three books to try and work out why they were so popular. I can only give my impression here.

I admire E.L. James massively. Quite how she captured so many people's imagination is beyond me: the characters are never fleshed out – bloody inner goddesses and biting her lip, and I never felt myself caring for them either. I did want to know how it all panned out, but I felt like I did about *The Hobbit* being three films. It should have been two films and *50 Shades* would have been much better as two books; they were too long, too repetitive and not very erotic. They were boring to any woman I have known to have an active and varied sex life and fascinating to women who have either led a sheltered life or have found their sex life dwindling as the marriage has gone on.

In one interview with the author, E.L. James does say that she has had many letters from women saying that she has saved or spiced up their marriage. This is a very good thing, but also highlights a lot of what has been said throughout this book, people just stop trying.

I have wondered how a woman goes from reading *50 Shades* and getting ideas about what she'd like her fella to do to her and for him to accept those ideas. If they've been having missionary position sex for the last five years and it lasts an average of 7 minutes and she says "Honey, I want you to tie me to the bed, spank me with a paddle and then play with my arse". It must have come as a hell of a shock to some and intimidated others who didn't know quite what to make of it all.

It reminds me of three girlfriends chatting in a pub one night. They were all talking about how to spice up their sex lives; to do something different.

Girl number one was the mistress and had been seeing her married lover for six months. Girl two had been seeing her boyfriend for nine months. Girl three had been married for eleven years. They all agreed that the next time they saw their men they would dress in mask, stockings, a basque and have a riding crop and would report back in a week. This they did.

"How did it go?" they asked simultaneously. Girl one reported first: "He loved it, he sucked my nipples for ages and we made love for an hour. It was brilliant." Girl two went next. "We were the same, he licked me like an animal and we were at it for over an hour. We'll be doing it again." They looked at the married woman. "Not quite the same effect for me," she said. "I was dressed just like we agreed and I thought I looked amazing. I'd even packed the kids off to my mums and waited for him to walk in the door after work. In he came, took one look at me, said 'What's for tea Zorro?' and slumped in front of the TV."

Even though this is a joke it does remind me of one of the ladies who took part in the sex survey. A very slim, pretty girl who has been with her husband for a few years, although they haven't been married very long.

When they were first together they couldn't keep their hands off each other, but gradually he reverted back to his natural state which is not that bothered about sex. The lady though is very highly sexed and constantly frustrated. She has even tried to tempt him in lingerie and the promise of an amazing evening of sex and he has turned her down claiming tiredness. As a dent to your self-esteem they don't come much bigger than that.

This lady is one of those who has turned to women as an alternative to unsatisfactory sex at home. If E.L. James has opened up the possibility of wild and crazy sex to many female readers (how many men have read the books? I only know of one other than me, although there must be more) at no time does she mention bisexuality or group sex. Both of which came up in the sex survey. One at a time though.

What is it about women that fascinate other women so much? I have to go from the research I have conducted on this, all based on conversations with friends, clients and friends of friends. All of them agree on one thing; curiosity was there long before any action was taken. That could have been originally stimulated by pornography or a conversation with girlfriends or partners past or present.

The first time I learnt of a bi-curious girl we had long conversations about what it would be like for her to sleep with another girl and whether or not I would be directly involved. She didn't want me to sleep with the other girl but she liked the idea that I would watch. I had to admit that the idea appealed to me as well. There was someone she fancied as well, but nothing ever happened. That initial question of "Would you like to sleep with me?" was always going to be a difficult one to ask and it never happened.

So why the curiosity? To me the first point is obvious, girls are lovely creatures, their bodies look nice, they feel great, so many women have soft skin and they mostly smell lovely too. What isn't there to like? And the bi-curious or bisexual agree. What they crave though, is real intimacy, the feeling of being made love to as well as having sex in decadent ways. As has been pointed out men are not very good at the preparation and after show parts of sex. Too often they are in too much of a hurry to either try and get the girl to orgasm or usually themselves. The kissing, touching and caressing isn't there and sometimes that is always the case.

One lady I spoke to said that whenever she had sex with her husband she was dry, by that I presume she meant she was lubricated in a minimal way, he pumped away until he had finished and then went about his business. She craved to be kissed (he was a terrible kisser, she said) and touched, to be desired.

One day the subject came up randomly about girls on girls and a drunken Saturday night turned into a love fest; it wasn't this lady's first sexual experience with a woman, but it was her friend's. It wasn't their last.

Having been friends for some time both were surprised by this turn of events, but both stayed with their husbands. It wasn't that they had gone off men (indeed both also had affairs as well), but they loved the contact they got from each other. Even the affairs didn't give them the intimacy they craved, the cuddling, the kissing, the talking, before and after sex that made them feel complete as lovers and as women. That was the irony, the affairs they had with men gave them the thrill of sex with someone new and exciting, but both stopped seeing the men because of their uncaring attitude. This may seem like wanting your cake and eating it, but the affair was supposed to make them feel better about themselves, not worse.

Another common factor is alcohol; this was present at almost every first experience ever mentioned and many of the follow up experiences as well. Dutch courage indeed. This lady's story illustrates this point more clearly.

A young mum, and married to a controlling husband for many years, she eventually found the courage to leave him taking her children with her. She was involved with a community who very much took her husband's side over the split and she found herself almost alone, without friends. Her sanctuary was that she had a house to herself and the children, with shared access she then found that she had time to herself and slowly, but surely she gained new friends who encouraged her to go out.

An attractive lady, she discovered that men were enamoured with her and she found that totally empowering. Her husband had always been one for keeping her down, eroding her confidence and making her believe that no one would ever look at her. As with the Emperor's New Clothes, when the truth was revealed the effect was startling. By her own admission for the first year she was 'a total slut' – her words; she has no idea how many men she slept with. What she did know was that she found her confidence and her voice, as it were. She found that she could control men with her skills in oral sex, she was fascinated by the teachings of the Far East and how they believed that semen gave them power.

This lady became a powerhouse, but as the year wore on she found, as so many do, that the sex was soulless and she began to wonder about some of her more attractive girlfriends. One night she had a girlfriend round for dinner, cooking being one of her interests, it was a weekend and much wine was consumed. As often happens in these situations the conversation turned more sexual, that moment occurs when a kiss seems the most natural thing to do and one kiss is usually all any situation takes to progress further.

The lady found that the experience left her feeling a lot more satisfied than she had with almost all of the men. The intimacy was there, a woman knows how to use her tongue far better than most men and there was that being held and kissed that she had craved too. Over the next couple of years there were other occasions with other ladies as she sought to experience what other women could do. She ended up sleeping with a few of her friends; one evening we were discussing these exploits – I found it all fascinating – because I wondered how you would know if a woman wanted to sleep with you. My experience with my ex-partner and that point of how you broached the big question seemed like a stumbling block to me.

Fortunately my friend revealed the secret, which was later backed up by other people telling me much the same thing. You have to manufacture the possibility of something happening. It's obvious really, when you think about it.

How do you 'manufacture' a situation? Remember, this isn't coercion in a negative sense, this is making something happen that you both want to happen but are worried of the possible embarrassment if it doesn't work out.

It's easy really, the girl is invited round to watch a movie, a catch up, possibly some hors d'oeuvres. The evening is a comfortable one, the ambience relaxed, wine is introduced, giggling begins, the conversation turns suggestive, a hand is placed upon a knee, it isn't removed, the moment of the first kiss comes and then proceedings take a natural course. Seduction in male-female and female-female is not so different.

I have also heard of a more direct approach working well. Two friends were at one of their homes and the husband was also there. Drink flowed, everyone was being generally silly and a random comment was thrown out by the husband. "I'd love to watch you two together. What do you think?" The answer was "Oh yes!" and then a most delightful show was put on.

The first thing that a man can learn from this is that girls like girls because of the same reason men like them, they are beautiful, they feel good and taste good, but what we should take from this is that women crave intimacy, romance and sensuality. It has been said many times now, men are often completely useless at all of this, or perhaps they get parts of it.

Some men think that a woman wants only the romance. They don't. They want a man to be understanding of their gentle natures but they also want a man to be a man. Things have evolved since our fathers' day and they are unrecognisable from our grandfathers' time; women want it all and if they don't get it they will keep looking. The days of marrying the boy next door and staying with him for 60 years are over. We live in a world of choice – that's true of electronics, of music, of shopping, of everything and it's true of relationships.

Social media (that's any form of website that puts us in touch with someone else from Facebook to Adult Friend Finder and Grindr) has put us out there. We post pictures, we tell the world of our interests and we want to be liked. We all look at friends' friends and see if there is anyone we like the look of or they might contact you out of the blue. If you accept that friendship then you have to be prepared for what happens. In the great majority of cases it is nothing, but sometimes your next partner has just appeared.

This book is about upping your game and you can take note or find yourself on your own. Women like women because they provide things that a man usually can't, but what do you do if you discover that your partner likes women? This depends very much on them, on you and where your relationship is going.

Many women discover later in their relationship that they are interested in women and struggle to find that outlet, but let us envision that one night the wife is out with some friends, they have a great night together, she is staying over at her friend's house and a scenario happens. Not only that, but both really enjoy it and want to repeat the process, when does the wife tell the husband or does the wife tell the husband? This all comes down to personal choice but writing from the male perspective how would you react if you found out that the wife you have known and loved for such a long time also has a bisexual side?

You could be outraged and hurt, I'm not sure where that would get you exactly, but it is an option. You could pretend it didn't happen, which makes about as much sense as being outraged. You could be intrigued, most men I know would definitely be interested. You might also feel a little insecure – is your wife likely to run off with this new lover? You might also feel insecure in your own performance, so many men fail in the oral sex department and to have a woman providing for your wife could shake your world.

You might want to watch – a fantasy for many men and the most common of all male fantasies, you might want to join in. If this is the case how does the other woman feel about that? If she doesn't like the idea what do you do then? Does she have her female lover but stay loyal to you where men are concerned? Do you class that as cheating on you and is it cheating if it is consensual? It requires a lot of thought and a lot of consideration. If the friend agrees to the threesome do you then have to agree to your wife having sex with another man, possibly the female lover's husband or partner?

This brings us into a new arena and option four – namely to introduce new sexual practices which could include swinging and/or dogging.

Key points to remember:

1   **The *Kinsey Report* of 1953 pointed the way to the future.**
2   **The *50 Shades of Grey* impact**
3   **Manufacturing a situation – friends and alcohol**
4   **Times have changed.**

Chapter 12
Shall we bring a friend?

All of this feels far removed from the image of relationships that we were brought up on: you meet a nice girl, you settle down, you have children, work hard, the children grow up, you build your pension, go on a couple of holidays a year, you get grandchildren, grow old together and eventually fade towards a happy demise.

It might have been that way for our grandparents but the world is now so different, so diverse, that nothing could be further from the truth. Of course some couples stay together for years, but none of us know how truly happy they are.

Whilst writing this book I have seen relationships from 15 to 30 years, and everything in between, falling apart and to everyone who knew them no one guessed how unhappy they were or more specifically how unhappy the woman was, because in every case the woman left the relationship. In different instances one lady chose the lesbian BDSM lifestyle, one left for a new relationship, one left because she couldn't stand being with her husband any longer and another left and not long after found herself in a new relationship, ironically with a married man. There are as many possibilities as there are stars in the sky.

For some people sharing each other sexually is how they keep their relationship fresh, exciting and, they will claim, loving. This brings us to option four, trying things you haven't tried before, that could be a visit to the local sex shop to buy toys or move on further from the girl on girl idea and enter the world of swinging and/or dogging.

One of the effects of *50 Shades of Grey* was that anything associated with the book also saw a boost in sales. Items such as handcuffs, paddles, masks and all manner of bondage gear was being snapped up in local sex shops and in *Ann Summers* chains (if you excuse the pun). The *50 Shades* effect perked up many a marriage but also the economy; E.L. James may have been the big winner, but it was difficult to see who (if anyone) lost out. Other authors such as Sylvia Day also benefitted as book shops and supermarket book shelves filled with 'mummy porn'. There was even a best-selling cd called the *50 Shades of Grey – The classical album* referencing music in the book.

The book changed the way many people thought about sex, it was ok for women to talk about it in a public way. Men had done this for years, but women have a tendency to talk about sex in a very direct, but intelligent way, whereas men so often fall into the stereotype that we have come to expect of them. This led to more open discussions about sex and it was clear that many women hadn't experienced anything like the things that Anastasia Steele went through; it was also clear that they wanted to see if they liked it. I found, in every case, that the more experienced the woman the less she saw in the book.

As I said, for me, it was hard work to get through the trilogy and I found the sex scenes exceptionally unerotic. To this day I am baffled as to why they took off as they did, but I am pleased that they sparked some form of sexual revolution.

Having read the *Story of O* and another widely read tome, *The Sexual Life of Catherine M* (a French book which was quite the sensation in its native land and across mainland Europe) I was surprised that at the root of the *50 Shades* story was a simple love story dressed up to be a sexual blockbuster. No other parties were introduced, no sex clubs were explored, it was all rather tame. The effect it had on its readers was not.

In the early years of the 21st Century a new word entered the English language: 'dogging'. I'm sure I first heard about it through a newspaper story, probably from a journalist who was outraged; I wasn't, I was intrigued.

At the time I was deeply entrenched in a settled relationship, but all things sexual interested us (although we had been monogamous) so we found this whole idea interesting and investigated further. Although the internet was not the giant it is today it was sufficiently well-versed that you could find all sorts of information online. Armed with this we set about finding out what we could. It seemed that two particular lay-bys on the road that linked Kettering and Northampton were renowned for dogging activity, although it also seemed that most of this was 'gay', not something we were interested in.

A friend of mine did tell me of a story where he was part of a spit roast with a girl there one afternoon; he the tail end and a complete stranger the other, but his was the only first-hand story I ever heard of there. We heard of all sorts of unusual locations (much later on I heard of one half a mile from the Northampton Town Football Stadium) – a car park, trees and somewhere dark seemed to do the trick.

Last year I pulled into a car park randomly and a couple of cars scurried away quite soon after, the feeling that I had disturbed a meet pervaded the place after they had driven away.

On to my only proper experience of dogging.

My then partner and I had no idea what to expect and only had half an idea of what the etiquette was; more to the point, we were pretty clueless, but excited and full of anticipation. We drove to the reservoir car park getting more excited as we got closer; what would we see? Would it be oral sex in the head lights, women being taken over car bonnets (as one lady told me she had been), or perhaps a queue of men waiting their turn whilst a lady was serviced one by one in the back of an Audi?

We drove in, there was a car parked at the far end of the car park with its lights off, so I backed into a parking space in the middle of the car park. I turned the engine off, the car headlights off and we sat in silence, barely daring to breathe. After a few minutes the car flashed its interior lights; I looked at my partner, she looked at me and I said, "What does that mean?" She said, "I can't remember."

At our first invitation to go and have a look we collapsed in giggles because we didn't know what the signal meant. Subsequently we found out that we had been invited to take a look. Like complete numpties we sat where we were. The other car stayed in darkness; after a few minutes their engine started and they drove off.

We sat in the car park alone. We weren't sure what to do so we stayed there to see if anything else would happen. It did. Two other cars came in and parked not far from us; our excitement levels went back up. After a few minutes a man in his mid-forties walked over to the car and came to my side. I wound down the window and we had a chat.

"What normally goes on here mate? It's the first time we've been."

"You never can tell," he said. "Sometimes there's a show on and sometimes it's as dead as a doornail. There was a nice show here last week, a girl did some guys over the picnic table."

A few weeks after this we went walking around the reservoir and I eyed the picnic table suspiciously. It didn't give up its secrets.

"Are you two up for anything?" the hopeful man asked.

"Not tonight, I don't think. We're here to look and learn," I dashed his hopes in two sentences.

"I'll wait around for a while then, see what happens," he said.

"Us too, seems a bit chilly out there," I mentioned, not very helpfully.

I closed the window and he wandered off.

I turned to my girlfriend. "What shall we do then?" I asked.

"Wait, obviously," she said and with that kicked off her shoes and put the seat back and reclined, so her feet were on the dashboard, she could see out of the windscreen and still be comfortable. She remained fully clothed.

I laughed, I knew exactly what she was doing and sure enough our new friend wandered back and this time went to the passenger side. We kept the windows firmly closed. He peered in and we tried not to piss ourselves laughing; it wasn't easy. He wandered off quite quickly having been disappointed.

No other cars came in whilst we were there and we decided enough was enough. We would try another time. I started the engine, my girlfriend put her seat up and we drove slowly out of the car park. About a week later there was a report in the local paper that the police had been called to investigate suspicious behaviour in the car park and they would be keeping an eye on the place. Our ardour was firmly dampened and we didn't go back to look again.

The laybys on the Kettering to Northampton road were visited a couple of times, but I never saw anything. One time we went through there with a couple of friends on the way to a night out; my girlfriend flashing the interior light furiously as we all laughed and told her to behave herself. Another time I drove through there on my own, out of curiosity; there were more cars travelling through the lay-by than there were on the main road and travelling about the same speed. I'm sure I heard that there was an accident one night as people criss-crossed the main road to get to each lay-by and the county council put up signs saying that the area was being watched. Perhaps it was as after a reported 'incident' all the trees were cut back, so it was no longer secluded from the road, and its notoriety began to fade.

But why would anyone want to have sex in the outdoors in front of strangers and more to the point with strangers? It all comes down to what turns people on and how they feel about the morality of sex.

Until 1800 sex wasn't always seen as an exclusive event, up until the late Middle Ages homes didn't have separate rooms as we know them now so everyone was in together. In some instances there might be a hung blanket separating you from other family members but often you were in a roundhouse together, or a Great Hall. Separate rooms, except for the exceptionally wealthy, didn't happen until the 14th Century so what you did people knew about and turned a blind eye. Of course, going back in time, before the Dark Ages in Britain, the Romans and the Greeks before them were known for the beautiful homes, but their parties, orgies and bath houses all went into historical legend.

The idea of public sex is certainly not new. Science, or rather developing science, was at the heart of a change in public opinion. With developments in what we understood about the human body the woman, culturally at least, became a vessel for the man to deposit his seed instead of a sexual being in her own right.

In Ancient Sparta a woman who could conceive was seen as just as important as a warrior male; without her the species could not continue. As the 18th Century became the 19th Century so the Victorian revolution started to the almost eternal damnation of sexuality ever since. It would take more than a hundred years before attitudes to sex finally relaxed.

The Victorians felt that sex should be a private thing that should be locked away behind closed doors lest minors and God knows who else were exposed to such dirty depraved acts. Prince Albert was one of the main proponents of this view, which was largely hypocritical as he and Queen Victoria could hardly keep their hands off each other. The irony that Edward VII (Queen Victoria's son) was seen as a philandering, whore chasing party animal led to his popularity when he succeeded his mother on her death in 1901 shouldn't be ignored. Just because authority and the Church think one thing doesn't mean the great majority have to agree.

The sexual revolution really began with the coming of the contraceptive pill and the obscenity trial of D.H. Lawrence's book, *Lady Chatterley's Lover*, in the 1960s the world seem to go sex mad for a while.

The 1967 Summer of Love, hippies and free love, all the way through the 1970s until the catastrophe of the AIDS epidemic in the 1980s. All of a sudden it seemed that having sex could get you killed. There were those who thought only the gay fraternity could catch HIV and then contract AIDS, but as education improved we all learned that this insidious disease would claim victims of all sexual persuasions. In time drugs would be developed that dramatically improved victims ability to fight HIV and many people would learn to live with the disease without it developing into AIDS and the epidemic seemed to pass somewhat, although whether that was more to do with more people taking precautions remains to be seen. It wouldn't be long before the sexual revolution was back on track again.

Pornography seemed to be the driving force this time; at one time difficult to get, its availability became easier and easier. In my teen years 'porn' was limited to the magazines of Paul Raymond, Hugh Hefner and Bob Guccione (*Penthouse*), with the advent of the scan magazine (*Private* being the most popular) so mainstream porn started to grow.

A scan magazine was a porn film in a magazine, the first one I ever saw was when a lad at school brought one in. This caused much fascination and amusement, the images sat in my brain for a very long time. In Soho in London, business was booming and in my late teens I would stroll around the streets with the windows proclaiming their wares, then one year all the windows were blacked out. Perhaps the Queen had visited, but more likely a by-law had been passed banning the blatant exhibits in the shop windows. Porn went back underground. Sex shops started opening in the provinces and were very popular, technology changed the playing field – digital technology changed the quality and the internet changed everything, just as it had with access to other people so it changed the access to porn.

More and more sites were appearing with greater access to free pornography. An early adopter of the technology was glamour model and soft porn star Danni Ashe, her site *Danni's Hard Drive* made her a millionaire and showed that boobs weren't her only talent. Porn had once been a great way for those so inclined to make money, but as the technology took over the access to free porn destroyed the money making capacity of the industry, in much the same way that Napster changed the way people bought, or rather didn't buy, music. The internet became awash with hardcore content.

Until Facebook and social media took over there were more searches and website hits for porn than anything else on the internet. The world was going sex mad. For young people this caused a problem as the age of innocence was disappearing rapidly, we all want our children to remain children for as long as possible, and images seen at a young age can have a dramatic effect, as well as affecting what you see as normal sexual practice.

In her book *Swingers – true confessions from today's swinging scene* the writer Ashley Lister describes the story of Mandy who inadvertently saw a porn film at the age of 9. She had got up early, no one was around so she pressed play on the video player expecting to watch *The Little Mermaid*. What she saw instead was a woman being double penetrated; as a little girl she couldn't work out what she was seeing at first, but an adult came flying down the stairs having heard the tell-tale signs of sex and turned the video off and admonished Mandy for being a bad girl.

The two experiences (the video and the telling off) stuck in her mind as both naughty and fascinating. At the age of 16 she had her first double penetrative sex, with two brothers, and became addicted to it. By her own admission "If I could find a man with two cocks I'd probably give up group sex."

As parents it is our job to protect children from such sites and images, but as they become young adults we know this is virtually impossible. They tend to be more cyber-savvy and can get around any parental controls that might be set and if they can't one of their friends can. With such access to porn does this tend to warp teenagers minds as to what is 'normal' sex? It would seem that it does – they seem to think that there is the pressure to act like a porn star, anal sex is seen as just as normal as vaginal, gangbangs are every teenage boys dream, the pressure for girls and boys to look like porn stars is both real and ridiculous.

The demise of Ron Jeremy as a porn star could be seen by some with regret; the rather portly, hairy, if well-endowed 'star' gave men hope everywhere that you didn't have to look like a junior version of Thor. How many teenage boys these days feel inadequate watching porn? The same can be said of girls, so many female porn stars either are slim and limber or surgically enhanced. How does this affect girls when they look at themselves? Yet another affirmation from a different media that they are not ideal?

However, this is an aside, for those who are not children or even burgeoning teenagers with a million fantasies porn has fuelled many a male mind and increasingly couples as well.

If *50 Shades* did anything it proved that there are a lot of horny women out there. Put them with horny men, porn as a stimulus and we see the rise and rise of swinging, in clubs, at home and at parties. Luisa Zissman, runner up in the 2013 *Apprentice* TV show, made no apologies for her participation in sex parties held in London and with that sex parties and swinging hit the public consciousness. Here was very attractive woman, on a top rated television show saying that sex parties were cool, they were fun to attend and there was nothing to be ashamed about. It was a very different picture than the one which had been painted in the lurid Sunday tabloids since the 1970s.

The People or the *News of the World* would often talk about 'sex dens' or 'perverts swapping wives' – everything was judgemental. Somewhat ironic that the *News of the World* would be closed down in 2012 because of its own behaviour.

Although she never revealed what went on at these parties, some of it came out when Luisa went into the *Celebrity Big Brother* house and revealed that she had slept with five men in one night. This outraged one of the younger contestants and a row ensued, with the male insisting that wasn't the way for a woman to behave.

These attitudes to sex are still revealing about modern society. Male excess has been known about, and sometimes celebrated, but it is seen as morally wrong to have the same attitudes and appetites. It doesn't take much thinking about to know that in the 21st Century this argument doesn't stack up. Not too much has changed since Kinsey revealed his report in 1953. Or has it? Other than much tut-tutting and a sharp intake of breath, Zissman's career hasn't been effected at all, some might say it has helped her career.

Look online and you will quickly find her name associated with "Killing Kittens" parties – so named because allegedly every time you masturbate somewhere a kitten dies. The world must be awash with deceased moggies if that's the case.

"Killing Kittens" is the brain child of Emma Sayle, a savvy young woman who set up the parties first in London and claims to have 40,000 UK members with parties attracting up to 250 people in London, as well as in Brighton and Manchester. At £100 a couple or £40 for a single girl this is big business. Miss Sayle's ambitions have now taken her to the US where she has held parties in New York and Los Angeles. Her rules are simple. All party goers must wear masks (pretty delicate things, not like something out of the Texas Chainsaw Massacre) No mask. No entry. Men must not approach women. Men must wait to be invited. Men must not look like they're flying solo. No means no. Only the kittens (women) can break the rules. No phones. Anything goes. The other stipulation is that you must be amongst the beautiful people; ages generally range from mid-twenties to late thirties although some older guys (in good shape) attend with younger women. This is definitely not the image of portly bellies, floppy boobs and saggy bums that the general public have in mind of a middle-aged orgy. "Killing Kittens" is the modern day Roman orgy complete with champagne and all the debauchery allowed.

If this is the high end of swinging then what is there for the ordinary couple who want to introduce other people into their sex lives? The answer is just about anything and anywhere you want.

In Birmingham exists 'Chameleons', the best club there is in the UK according to Mark Brendon, the author of *Swinging – the games your neighbours play*. A most extensive and exhaustive book covering every facet there is of this sub-division of sexuality. Brendon spent three years swinging. He starts by explaining that he has led a mostly vanilla lifestyle with only eight threesomes in his life, three where he was one of two men and the others where it was him and two women. I would suggest that isn't a vanilla lifestyle and that even before he dipped his toe, and anything else, into the swinging world he was ahead of most people. A threesome with two women is most men's dream, a fantasy that most never fulfil. Some people have said that having experienced their fantasies they wished they had left them as fantasies. Others found that reality far exceeded even their wildest dreams. I guess it all comes down to the people who are playing.

In the sex survey there were a few people who describe their experiences as part of a threesome, or in being the subject of a gangbang and to most people, again, this is way beyond what most people will ever experience. For some people this behaviour is so depraved, so base, as to find the whole idea abhorrent. For others it fuels the fantasy.

Back to *Swingers – true confessions from today's swinging scene* by Ashley Lister is the story of Eve and Frank. This couple began by dogging in a sedate fashion, if such a thing were possible, until the night when Eve decided she wanted to be taken by 12 strangers in one night. With a healthy supply of condoms and stamina to match things began in a wave of sex and continued until she could barely walk. By her own admission she lost all sense of time and place after her husband Frank kissed her as she was being taken doggy style by an unknown guy. It was this kiss more than anything that sent her into raptures of orgiastic fever. The day after she struggled to walk and she was sore for a week, but Eve loved the experience and they claim that it brought them closer together.

All over the UK there are places where dogging is going on, probably as you read this now, and for those who prefer the indoors there are sex clubs like 'Chameleons'. Mark Brendon visited most and all have different things to offer, so what would you expect?

There will be a reception area (all clubs demand ID in a photographic form to new members), fees range from £20 for single girls up to £70 for single guys. Most clubs will have a specific night when single men are allowed, it seems to be Friday in most places, and couples plus single girls on Saturday nights. There will be a bar and dance floor, although many clubs don't have a drinks licence so you are encouraged to bring your own.

In truth most people don't drink too much as the purpose of these clubs is to have sex, whereas in a normal club it is to dance and to find someone to take home to have sex with; the problems caused by excess alcohol wouldn't be welcome in a sex club either. There will be different small play rooms, sometimes dark and sometimes with a window so that people can watch you and others.

There is always at least one massive bed where eight couples can mix and mingle, usually a Jacuzzi, sometimes a pool and/or a sauna and a dungeon of some kind. Sometimes with a cross that a person can be tied to, more popular since *50 Shades* talked about them in the 'Red Room of Pain' complete with flogging tools, paddles and sometimes a sex swing. Of course, the equipment isn't any good without the people to play and if they are not of 'Killing Kittens' quality what are they like? Again, according to

Brendon the ages at which people swing are from 28-60, with the average being 40. It also said that people do come in all shapes and sizes and whilst dark rooms may be good for beginners who are shy, the downside is you never quite know who you might be sharing a room with and who you might find nuzzling on your jewels. Far better, to stay in the light (dim as it may be) and know what you are letting yourself in for or what you might like.

The etiquette, whether at a private party or in a club, is always congenial. The novice is always understandably nervous, and there is no obligation to join in.

Rules are usually established before a couple visits for the first time, but in the heat of the moment these are often crossed or broken, but with permission. The point about swinging is to bring a couple closer together by accepting sex as a sensual activity and that both parties come away with a heightened experience. It is often said that the best sex for the couple is when they get home or to their hotel room for the night; the reason for this is that sex is a physical act whilst making love involves all the chemical reactions that you were trying to remember by going swinging in the first place. In other words, for you to feel physically about each other as you did when you fell in love.

There will be many of you reading this who will be struggling with this concept and that's because we've all been brought up the same way: sex is between one man and one woman, but clearly it isn't. The sex survey proved that, you know by talking to your friends that isn't true and to think that it is would be madness. There are as many combinations of people as you can think.

A funny experience I had once on a training camp I was teaching on was that I was with my girlfriend, and a few of the students whilst we had lunch. The camp was in Germany, the food was pretty bad, but the company was excellent. There was a Parisian guy who now lived in French

Polynesia and all week we had been wondering which one of the two identical girls he was walking around with was his wife or girlfriend and as he was on his own at lunch that particular day I thought this the right time to ask.

"Which of those girls are you with?" I asked politely.

"Both," came his reply. Around the table forks stopped being lifted to mouths, chewing stopped and we all looked at each other. He continued. "I married both of them; in Polynesia this is quite normal."

"Oh," I said and looked at my Belgian friend across the table. "How would you feel about two wives Jean?" (name changed). Knowing full well that he had been married for twenty years then.

"No," he said, shaking his head, "One is quite enough."

We were shocked though, because it was outside of our normal experience; you can't say it's wrong if it works in the Pacific Ocean, but then they were never exposed to the ethics of Victorian Britain and its Colonies. Queen Victoria certainly knew of love with Prince Albert, but with his passing in 1861 at the age of 42 a dark cloud came over the lands. That cloud was piety. The queen was rightly devastated and led the rest of her life in mourning, this was terrible for her and even worse for Britain and the Empire. The old lady lived for another forty years influencing the social climate of the time, when sex became a taboo subject; she seemed to forget that she had nine children!

With the Jack the Ripper murders of 1888, sex got another slap as it was obviously a deranged pervert killing these prostitutes – and why do men need prostitutes? Because they couldn't ask for 'perverted' sexual acts from their wives, therefore, all men are perverts and all women are sluts, so it seemed to say. It would take a long time for attitudes to change.

We discussed earlier in the book the historical timeline of how things progressed but morality wasn't discussed. The fact is that there are many people who love the idea of having sex with lots of people, whether that is one at a time or with many people at once.

Rock stars are idolised because of the groupies that flock to them; two stories I remember are as follows. In 1968 when Jimi Hendrix returned to the USA he was found in bed one morning with ten women, for some people that is going to be the ultimate fantasy. The other story concerns Elvis Presley; he was on furlough whilst in the Army and as was his habit he was in Paris. He received a phone call one afternoon at his hotel room from the Moulin Rouge who enquired as to whether Mr Presley might kindly allow the girls back to work as they had a show on that evening. This was twenty to thirty girls for Elvis and his few friends. Upon such stories are legends built. It's not only the men though; in the 1920's the story was that Clara Bow, a silent movie star, once slept with an entire US football team. How true these stories are is hard to tell, but the fact is the public are fascinated by such things and when it seems that such opportunities are available some people will indulge.

Sex clubs have greedy girl nights, where a girl will have as many men as possible orgasm over her; there are amateur porn sites where men can sign up to be one of the bit part players to the greedy girls fantasy. Killing Kittens aren't the only sex parties; it seems that every weekend you can indulge any fantasy for only a few pounds and a form of ID.

Back to Mark Brendon and his experiences. Ab-Fab parties near Heathrow was one of his favourite places to visit. Different to a sex club, the parties were held in the hosts somewhat large house which has two dungeon rooms, a Jacuzzi, a swimming pool, two dancing areas and amongst the play rooms a spider room, where a person can be tied to a spider's web. The host's job at a party is to make sure everyone leaves having had a good time. Brendon certainly thought that the best parties were held here.

For all the debauchery on offer, and it is interesting to think that whilst you are watching *Britain's Got Talent* or *X Factor* and eating a curry there are thousands of people all over the country (let alone the world) who are engaging in group sex and becoming porn stars in their own right. There are so many of my friends who have told me that sex stops when the children come along in a marriage and yet evidence would suggest that it isn't true for many people.

Even as you read this I know you are thinking 'but why would I want to watch my wife/partner getting fucked by one or more strangers?' There is a simple answer to this, there exist in this world 'watchers', people who love to watch their partner being taken on a journey that one person alone can't take them on. Equally there are people who get turned on by watching their woman, or man, have sex with other people. What you think is largely irrelevant unless you want to take part. If it works for other people then it works for them. Many swinging couples will swear by the mantra "those who swing together stay together." For them it brings them together and whether you approve or not is of no interest to them at all.

For those who are now intrigued here are some guidelines and thoughts. If it is the man who thinks that this will be a good idea, and the woman agrees, you have to bear in mind a very important fact. Women, by and large, do not fade through the night. A man is mostly wasted after 30-45 minutes of vigorous fornicating and licking and once his orgasm is over he has to wait a while before he's ready to go again. This is not true of the woman, unless she is so sore she can no longer continue.

This can cause some problems – one couple I know of went to a club where they met another couple they had arranged to meet. The husband was finished in the normal time period, whereas the other man had more stamina and was more into his swapped wife than the first husband had been. Although they had taken private rooms having your partner knocking on the door asking you to hurry up is not good etiquette in this type of place. The wife was still curious and wanted to watch more of the action, but was hauled away in rather unceremonious fashion by the now jealous husband, which leads rather obviously into understanding jealousy.

For most of us it is an emotion that we feel when someone else wants our partner or we perceive that to be the case. However, if you go to a sex party or a sex club it is pretty obvious that you are offering up your partner to have sex with someone else. Imagine the embarrassment if no one wanted you or her. It's worse than not being picked for the school hockey or football team. However, should they be picked then how do you cope? Sage advice from Brendon again: "Expect it. You will get jolts or twinges … but take each other's hand, smile, express pride … Become too engrossed in your own pleasure and you run the risk of losing not only your future in the 'lifestyle' but your partner into the bargain."

Again for some it is a step too far, too much for a normal relationship to experience and also of course what of the safety aspect. Won't you catch something? A final word from Mr Brendon. "Oral sex is, of course, invariably performed without condoms. Penetrative sex, however, is always protected. When a man is moving from woman to woman, even when the two of them are muzzle to groin, he must change the condom every time. I have used twenty or more in an evening with just three girls. Sex toys are also cleaned between uses." It would seem that safety is of the utmost importance and it is in your interests to make sure you abide by these rules if you were to partake.

What of homosexuality, bisexuality and lesbian trysts? It would appear that 80% of ladies who attend such events are bisexual and partake of both sexes at an event. For men it is rare; they will of course, have their own parties to attend. There is also that feeling of what will it be like for you to be one end of your wife whilst someone else is at the other end, or even the staple of porn, the double penetration? Is the rear entrance saved for you only or do you share that also?

From reading Brendon's book a couple of times it would appear that even if there are rules to begin with these often change in the heat of the moment. What must remain is trust. Without trust this scene should be avoided at all costs; if you are going into this area to bring yourselves closer to that lusty, crazy couple you once were it would seem for some people that this works.

It is also true that when things are shaky this is something to be avoided. Sex does not bring two strangers together who were once lovers; it does bring strangers together to become lovers.

Key points to remember:

1	**The *50 Shades* effect**
2	**Dogging – the rise and the reality**
3	**A short history of sexual liberation**
4	**Swinging – it's more popular than you might think**
5	**'Killing Kittens' and 'Chameleons'**
6	**What you might see, or experience, at a club or party**
7	**Guidelines, thoughts and safety**

Chapter 13
What else could there be?

It would seem that we have exhausted every sexual aspect there is to bring life into this tired relationship, so what else is there? This is a simple answer, everything else; the world is full of myriad possibilities.

This book was written with a particular age range in mind, a large age range mind you, but I thought from the start that most people who read this would be from thirty to fifty years old, the ages at which marriages start to fall apart. That is not to say, however, that if you met someone at 18, you wouldn't be sick of them by 23 and want to move on, or at any other point in your twenties.

When we become ingrained in who we are and forget who we once were; it doesn't have to be this way, but it often is. When I ran my therapy practice people would sometimes arrive in quite a dreadful state; I was often seen as the last chance for a ruined relationship and it has to be said more people came to the realisation that their marriage was over than walked away stronger. Why? Because they had left it so late.

When someone sits in front of you with tears streaming down her face for the best part of an hour and you realise it's not because she is sad the relationship it is over, these are tears of frustration for staying in a place which she'd wish she'd left a long time before. When I was younger (especially in the 1960s and 1970s) many couples stayed together for the children, most people realise now this isn't the best way for the children to grow up happy.

Start gently: talk to each other, about subjects other than work, the kids and family. This completely confuses some people because this is all they talk about and encapsulates why there are problems. When you first met you didn't talk about children and your mum and dad. You began to learn about each other, your likes, your dislikes, what fascinates you, what repulses you. How close are you intellectually? How far apart are you philosophically? These were the types of questions you asked when you first met and look how much you've changed in the intervening years.

I have had husbands tell me that he talks to his wife every day, but when I have spoken to the wife she will tell me that he talks about work, football and the kids. She is starved of intellectual conversation and she is going to be turned on by the person who can provide it. She doesn't want in depth discussions on shoes, fashion or handbags, that's what girlfriends are for, she wants you to stimulate her brain. If you do that you will stimulate your heart and we return back to sex, it will improve naturally and even more importantly we return to connection.

Once you have established common ground then decide what you are going to do about it. Some girls love cars, whether it's a VW Bugfest, the Goodwood Festival of Speed or an Italian car meet. Find out when the meets are on and take her. Other girls love music; I'm not talking about dancing (although that is good too), I mean they 'love' music. They have extensive music collections and they are looking for the next new sound to excite the ears. Music is a fantastic opportunity to bond; listening to music in the dark, wrapped in each other's arms, is the perfect way to reconnect, and indeed connect, if it's a new relationship. To have laid in the dark snuggled close together listening to *Shine on you crazy diamond* by Pink Floyd, *Chasing Cars* by Snow Patrol or *Sexual Healing* by Marvin Gaye will always put you in the mood, but it doesn't have to be about sex. It's the holding, the kissing, talking softly or just lying there together lost in your thoughts, about each other, not worrying that the cat needs feeding or what time you have to be up to drive to Bradford in the morning. To be is enough.

Take time to have weekends away or at the very least days out, without children. The Lake District is a perfect weekend getaway, to stay in your hotel and explore each other or to get out into that wonderful scenery and walk the hills, go to Keswick, visit the Beatrix Potter Museum or drive around the magnificent lakes. Snowdonia is another gorgeous location and if you're going to go that way take time to visit Portmerion, the quirkiest place in Britain and where *The Prisoner* was filmed in the 1960s.

For days out walk in the Peak District, visit London and make a plan. No more than three museums, plenty of time to take in the sights or if you book far enough in advance Tea at the Ritz. Over-priced, but an experience that will stay with you forever.

Join English Heritage or the National Trust and find out more about this wonderful country we live in. So many people travel abroad without knowing the beauty that exists in their own homeland. People often say that they are bored, that there is nothing to do; people who say this are boring and lack imagination. If you have someone like this in your life get rid of them, they will sap the life out of you.

Some people will complain that 'everything' is too expensive. One answer to this is improve your financial situation: if you don't like your job, change it; if you don't have a job, get one; if your business isn't doing well enough, stop messing about and make it more successful.

If that's not possible in the short term go for a walk; where I live there is a valley a three minute walk away, but if you don't have such immediate access to the countryside drive a short distance to find it or if you're in a town walk the streets. Charles Dickens was an avid walker and would walk for up to five hours a day. Charles Darwin would walk three times a day for between twenty and thirty minutes and wrote voraciously; they found the fresh air kept the mind stimulated. Walking will also give you plenty of opportunity to talk or to think; one girlfriend and I used to go out every weekend for walks of up to twenty three miles; a bit excessive, but it gave us lots to discuss.

By now I hope you're getting the idea; it may have seemed to some of you that I am obsessed with sex and that sex is the only thing you need to get right in order to stay together. I don't think that at all, I do think if the sex is terrible at the beginning you're on to a tough ask from the start, but relationships are about the whole package.

You have to fancy each other, you have to find each other funny, stimulating, interesting, a joy to be around or you fall into the habit that so many couples fall into – comfort and mediocrity and we then find ourselves back at the beginning again. You have to be a fun person, an interesting person, someone that other people want to spend time with.

Men that women like have all of these qualities; too often a bloke will be swayed by a beautiful smile, a tanned thigh, a heaving bosom or a flick of the hair.

Beauty is in the eye of the beholder, but it is also in the heart and brain of a person. A beautiful woman who cannot converse soon loses her appeal, this is also true of men.

If the body stimulates you, but the mind dulls you to the core you will find yourself looking for another tattooed bad boy soon enough.

Key points to remember:

1   **There is more to life than sex!**
2   **If you want help to save your marriage don't wait until it is too late**
3   **Start talking, in depth, about everything**
4   **There are endless things to do**

Chapter 14
It's time to go

Which finally brings us back to option six, walking away.

We began with this option and some will say let him go, why waste all that time and effort on him in the first place? Remember you can take option one at any time in the process, but let's examine how far you will have travelled and how long it might take as well. Some relationships fall apart almost from the start and yet still people get married; I've known a few people who said that they should never have married their husbands, so why the bloody hell did they do it? Peer pressure is a big thing. If you've spent eighteen months planning a wedding and in the last three months you start to wonder why, it's still difficult to say to your friends and parents that you don't want to go through with it.

As part of the research for this book I watched a whole heap of romantic movies and chic flicks, one of them being *Runaway Bride*. For those who haven't seen it Richard Gere finally helps the runaway bride settle down when she discovers what it's like to be herself, without the pressure of other people expecting too much of her. In the public arena at least; my advice: if it doesn't feel right, don't do it. Somewhere along the line this isn't going to work out.

Another thing that couples do to try and stay together is to have children; this has to rate as the maddest thing you can possibly do. Children are wonderful, but can also be expensive, time consuming and energy draining. The only way to enter into parenthood is when you are totally committed to each other. Children are not sticking plasters to fix or heal a failing relationship. Anything else will lead to the couple becoming further and further apart and more children with weekends in different houses becoming the norm. Having said this, if you do split up this can be a really good thing for the children.

When couples stay together 'for the kids', those children will invariably grow up in a household either strained by keeping up appearances, or surrounded by negativity, arguments and sometimes, abuse. By being apart both sets of parents can concentrate on the act of parenting; spending more quality time with the children and bringing them up in a happier home. It takes intelligence and patience from the parents, but the rewards are worth it.

What of the feelings of the parents when another man or woman is introduced into the equation? I wondered this when my son's mother and I split; at first, as a man you wonder if you will be usurped in the pecking order, not something you want to happen. This didn't happen because I saw my son at least twice a week and stayed in contact; he never forgot who his dad is. This contrasted dramatically with my experience as I didn't see my father for over twenty years, from the time my mother re-married until I saw him in my late twenties. I call my stepfather 'Dad', and still do.

As adults it is your responsibility to make sure your children grow up as happily as they can. Even if you find yourself not being able to stand the sight of each other (how does that happen when you were once so in love?) you still have to be civil in front of the children or you just pass on your prejudices to another generation.

It's easy to read here, but far more difficult to do, particularly if you feel you have been wronged; perhaps you found out she or he was having an affair and you want to keep the children away from the despicable person. Understandable, but who wins and who loses? No one wins and everyone loses. By all means take out your wrath on the perpetrator, but spare the children your vitriol. It will be rewarded when they are teenagers and adults.

Anyway, we are now at the leaving section; Let us review. You originally thought you would leave your husband or wife/partner, but wanted to give it every chance possible of keeping it together. One of the biggest challenges here is that often couples still love each other, but in a brotherly-sisterly way i.e. they are close, but no longer physically attracted to each other. This leads to all sorts of guilt; they may still be a really good friend to you and you don't want to hurt them, but the fact remains that to stay together will leave you with a whole heap of regret.

You may also wonder if parting will bring regret; what if you are wrong? What if the grass on the other side is mud and swamp? There's a very simple way of working this through in your head.

Tony Robbins calls this the 'rocking chair' test. I want you to imagine being around 80 years of age and you are looking back on your life; you may still have another twenty years to go, but at 80 it would be fair to assume that you would feel in a reflective mood. I want you to think about the person you are now with (if this doesn't relate to you now then either think back or imagine your future) and think of the things that have made you read this book in the first place. These are the things I've heard as I've researched this book:

"The sex is awful. He thinks a couple of minutes in the morning is alright, that sometime I'm going to be satisfied with that. I just get going and he's finished and making the tea."

"He's never bloody happy; there's always something wrong with him. Job is shit, life is shit, the kids don't respect him. He does my bloody head in."

"When he tries to make love to me nothing happens. I've told him to see a sex therapist or a doctor, anyone, but he won't. Instead he paws me, tries to get me horny, I try too and then it hangs there, limp and fucking useless. Nothing can make you feel less desired than a limp cock attached to a man who you find unattractive."

"We've never got any money. That's his mantra. It's always been like this, for years. I tell him to get another job and he tells me there are none out there."

"He always has time for everyone except me. We spend so much time keeping every other bugger happy that we don't have any time for ourselves, although now I'm rather glad of it and I just go out with my friends."

"Work and money, that's all he ever talks about. I try to talk about other things, but no, that's it. Work and money. It's not that we're hard up, we do ok, but there has to be more to life than this."

Men also complain though.

"She really doesn't have a clue. I work my bollocks off trying to bring up the kids right and make sure we have a good life and all she does is moan. I wonder why I bother."

"I have all these fantasies I'd like to try, but how do I tell her? She'll think I'm a total bloody perv. Actually I might be, but how do I tell her?"

Men might also want to experience gay sex (Grindr etc), but whatever is happening whether from the male or female side, this relationship is finished. Without trust, without communication, without sexual compatibility what else is there? You have the shell of a relationship and you are kidding yourselves that you are going to stay together. It is time one of you left.

Now comes the hard part. The saying "It's over."

I've done it enough times and it is always horrible, there are always tears and always pain. I've had it done to me as well, my heart has broken and I have wanted to die. It's got easier to deal with as I've become older, not because the pain is any less, if anything it's worse, but I know I'll come through it. I know something else will happen, I will meet someone else, something in my life will change. Life will go on. Some people doubt this to be true.

I believe in fairytales, true love, love at first sight and the work needed to make a relationship successful. It's why I wrote the book, but it would be remiss of me not to talk about the end of a relationship – and more importantly to write about the end before the end of the book. As I said, there is more to tell yet.

Let's go through both parts of the process, first telling them it's over and then how to cope when it happens to you.

Telling someone you don't want to be with them anymore is downright horrible, it doesn't matter if you've been with them for a month or twenty years, it's still upsetting. What you are saying to that person is "I reject you in every way possible." Who wants to be told that? If being told that someone loves you is the one of the best feelings in the world then telling them you don't love them and don't want to be with them is one of the worst. I've hated it every time I've had to do it.

When you do it after a short amount of time (two weeks to three months) you will often hear the plea "You haven't given it enough time." The truth is that you have. We instinctively know when we want to spend more time with someone and we also know when we want to spend less, or no, time with someone.

Love is all about chemicals; the serotonin, the dopamine, the testosterone, everything that another person can cause in you. When those chemicals aren't released then you know it's over. A few times I have had the sensation of being in bed with someone and wishing I wasn't there. This is a disaster, for you and for them. You have to get out of that situation as soon as possible. To prolong it will only cause more pain for both of you. This is where courage is needed, to face the other person's pain and possible disappointment or anger and get it over with sooner rather than later.

Many years ago I read a quote in Robin Norwoods's book *Women who love too much*. It was this: "the only pain you can avoid is the pain of avoiding pain." I can remember exactly where I was when I read that, on a break from a fork-life driving course of all things, and I sat there trying to work out what it meant. Three times I re-read it until it finally dawned on me, the only thing you can avoid is the pain, or worry, of not doing a thing. It has to be done, so do it. To procrastinate further causes more pain – the other person will sense that something is wrong and then they worry about what you are going to say whilst you worry about what you will say and how they will take it. That part isn't really your concern except in helping them to understand that it is over.

A person may ask you to reconsider, they may deny you have told them, they may cry, they may get angry, hopefully they won't become violent – to you or themselves, they may deny it is happening. They almost certainly will feel extreme pain and there is nothing you can do about that. Remember in this process we have gone through six steps; it's not like you woke up one morning, thought "sod it, that loser can piss off", you have agonized to get to this moment, but this moment must be taken or you will find yourself unhappily rocking in the rocking chair wondering why you wasted your life. Above all you must stick to your decision, no matter what their reaction and to do this you must plan ahead or risk being dragged back into situations you don't want to happen.

Are you leaving them or are you asking them to leave? If you are leaving make sure everything is done to get your things, otherwise you'll find yourself never wanting to go back.

Even at such painful times there are still humorous moments. A friend of mine once told me that she had discovered that her fella had been cheating on her. She bided her time and waited until he was out at work one day; she cleared the flat they shared of every piece of furniture except for the kettle. She left him this in the middle of the living room floor, but she took the electric lead with her!

In a lot of relationships you can sit down, discuss the future and agree to part amicably, in some that isn't possible. You have to know the situation.

Personally I'd always recommend against doing a disappearing act whilst your partner is at work, but sometimes that's the only way it can be done. If children are involved, and they often are, then I feel it's important to make the party left that they know their place in the children's lives. No mother can be replaced and nor can a father.

Even though my dad was hopeless I still thought of him as my father, but it was my stepfather who was 'Dad'. The same thing was true of when I became the in-house parent with my stepsons. They never called me 'Dad', it was always by my name, but we have a bond that exists to this day. At first I was worried that my son would relate to his mother's boyfriends (and now, her husband) as dad but that never happened.

It comes down to the same thing again – communication. Keep talking to each other; nonviolent communication that I talked earlier in this book definitely helps. Understanding which needs aren't being met and the emotions associated with those unmet needs.

Also asking the question "What does this mean to me?" helps. Eventually you get to the real answer. If you don't do a runner then there is only one way to tell someone that you are leaving.

Be honest.

You have fallen out of love; it happened a long time ago and there is no chance of you changing. You have to leave as you are wasting yours and his (her) life by staying. It is time for both of you to find new challenges. At this point you will often get an objection – that they don't want you to leave, but you have to be firm, despite tears or tantrums.

Once you have decided on this course of action then you must carry it through. To capitulate now would only lead to more pain and suffering in the future. As I have grown older I have become better at ending relationships that were going nowhere. In every situation the other person was lovely, in some cases it would seem perfect for me in every way and yet that indefinable aspect was missing – chemistry. If you're not in love you are in 'like' and 'like' will not sustain a relationship. Sometimes the sex was good too, but what you are looking for is the total melding of mind, body and spirit and to surrender to anything less is a waste of your time and theirs. Much better to end something early than spend three years on it as I did when I was younger. Now I know exactly what I want from a person and this helps with making decisions as well.

The moment of telling them is, of course, the hardest, but you have to put yourself in an emotional bubble. To say the words, know the meaning, accept the consequences and be on your way. Almost as if it isn't you saying the words, if you are swayed by their emotions then often you will be lost. They may think you cold or unfeeling and they may tell their friends after that you are a cold hearted bitch (or the male equivalent), but none of this is important. All that is important is for you to get out of the situation.

What other people think is irrelevant; you may be the gossip of the community or the school yard for a while, but soon enough another catastrophe will occur and you will be forgotten. To forge your new life is your only concern, remember, it took a long time to get to this sad situation. Bruce Lee, the martial arts movie star, had a great phrase he used to use in times of difficulty: "Walk on." It is a phrase well remembered.

That's if you have to say it, how do you cope if you are the one who has had it said to you? I have heard all sorts of things this year, about how people would cope if their long term relationship was to finish. People have said they would die without their partner; people have said they wouldn't know how to cope, people have said there would be nothing left to live for and they would rather commit suicide than go on without them. These are all controlling mechanisms. You are saying that the only way you can get a woman (let's go with the male perspective as it is by far more women who leave men than the other way around as we have established) to stay with you is to tell her that you would kill yourself if she doesn't stay with you.

This woman has agonised over how she is going to leave you because you are impossible to live with and now you want to lay your death at her feet. No wonder she's going to leave you. It's time to act like a grown up, not a spoilt child. If you're in pain as you read this you might struggle with this section, but please stay with me. Do you think I have never had my heart broken? It has happened a number of times, the last time the worst of all, but I came through all that pain wiser and more focussed on who I wanted in my life.

It first happened when I was 19, I thought I was in love with someone and she went off with someone at a party; we'd been together just over a year at that time. The party was on a Saturday night in April, I found her slightly stoned and snogging a bloke in one of the bedrooms and I got mad and stormed out of the house expecting her to follow me. She didn't. Then I felt even more stupid. The following day I went to see her and she said it was over with us. I was devastated, heartbroken; it was the worst pain I had ever felt. I can't remember the rest of the day, but I do remember the Monday morning at work. I was morose, depressed, broken. I worked in a fast food place then and trying to be pleasant to people was not what I wanted to do. Throughout that day my heart hurt, but somehow I got through it. I did what everyone does at times like this. I found the most miserable music I could find and I listened to it incessantly.

Phil Collins was at the height of his powers in the early 1980s and *If leaving me is easy* became my constant companion, I played it over and over again. In fact, that album *Face Value* was the one I listened to the most. All the broken-hearted people of the world helped to make Phil Collins rich as he talked our language, which made sense as the album was written about his first divorce.

Monday became Tuesday and I felt a little better, all cried out and emotionally numb. I added weight training to my fitness regime and whilst I worked out the emotional pain didn't hurt as much, but after the workout the pain came again. If only I could train every hour.

Tuesday became Wednesday and I could feel a change coming over me. Instead of being sad I could feel my anger rising. I began to realise that I was the one feeling the pain, but she was the one who had gone off with another bloke at the party. I may have been a fool, but at least I didn't cheat on her under her very nose. Anger began to rise. I was pissed off, really pissed off. I was being treated like a mug and she was getting away with it. I began to understand how crimes of passion occur – when you feel so used that you want to kill someone else.

The point is though that you know it's your own fault. The love is no longer a two way street and if that's true then you must bear 50% of the blame. She is with someone else because you didn't treat her right. I was young then and didn't understand this. I thought the world was unfair; I didn't understand then that if you don't focus on something you can't be surprised if it disappears. That's as true for business as it is for relationships and friendships. Remember that old NLP adage? If you want something then you have to go first. If you want more love then you have to give it first. If you want neglect then show it to the person you claim you love.

As days passed so the feelings of loss passed as well. I threw myself whole heartedly into training, entering half marathons and marathons and I found that physical fitness replaced those feelings of serotonin that I had found from the relationship. The postscript to this little story is that we got back together after some months, then we bought a house together, but ultimately it didn't work out. She met someone, so did I and for a long time we didn't see each other, but the magic of Facebook brought us together and she is now one of my longest standing friends. And the irony is I realised I was never in love with her at all, I just thought I was, although that's not to say that I didn't care very deeply for her. I would learn this when my heart was broken the next time.

This was the girl who told me she didn't love me on that May bank holiday and was gone by the weekend. This was entirely my fault. I had known something was wrong for a while, but I thought we'd always be together; we'd split up so many times and got back together that I thought that's the way it would always be, I hadn't realised I'd pushed her too far. I was devastated when she left. I saw her in a club about six weeks after she left me; she was with another bloke and I was heartbroken; not only that but she looked amazing. It was tough, but I got through it.

My longest relationship had a number of separations and near endings before we finally called it a day; I thought about her for a long time after wondering if I had been right to leave, but it all worked out in the end. The worst of all though was the relationship before the one I am in now. That nearly broke me, although in essence it was also the catalyst for me to finally start writing.

This was a crazy love affair, mad about each other, but never able to keep it together. After nearly two years of on and off we decided that we were settled enough to rent a place together. It all went horribly wrong though and she left me the week before Christmas. I can truly say that it was the worst Christmas ever. My son stayed with me, a friend stayed overnight to keep me company, but I was inconsolable. I didn't realise it at the time but I was completely emotionally broken. I did my best to keep my mind off the situation; I went on lots of dates, I trained, watched *Rocky* movies and Billy Connolly videos. I did everything that I had learnt from NLP, nonviolent communication and self-hypnosis. What worked in the end though was time; just letting enough time pass to realise that one day it would work out.

At no time did I think I wanted to kill myself and I certainly never told any of the girls who broke my heart that I would do so. Dignity is something easily lost and once gone cannot be replaced; people remember if you have an angry fit in front of them or smash something up or worse, threaten other people. No matter how much pain you are in you must retain your dignity.

You will go through the stages of loss, fear, loneliness, anger and loathing, but you will come out the other end hopefully a wiser man.

There are two reasons why a woman leaves you. Either she's cold hearted (in your mind at least) and you're better off without her or you made mistake after mistake. You didn't make her feel like a princess and you have to expect these things to happen.

I have never, ever, understood men who moan about their wives or girlfriends at home. If she is such a moaner, leave her; I suspect though that you know where your bread is buttered and you are lucky to have her.

I have a simple rule for a successful relationship; you treat her like a princess and she has to treat you like a prince. If you do that then neither of you will ever have to look at anyone else; if you don't you will get everything you deserve.

Key points to remember:

1	**Children should never be used as pawns in your troubles**
2	**Common complaints about each other**
3	**Telling the other person it's over**
4	**Understanding your role as a parent**
5	**Keeping calm, without threats**
6	**It's happened to me too**
7	**Keep your dignity**

Chapter 15
Sleeping With The Enemy

The subject of domestic abuse took me somewhat by surprise as I wrote the book. Various partners over the years had told me about physical abuse they had suffered, but few talked about mental cruelty. In therapy sessions it wasn't discussed much either, but in the 18 months of researching and writing I heard more and more examples of how women were being controlled.

Domestic abuse isn't obvious either because the women become such good actresses as well, putting on a smile and going about their business. We recognise a bruise when we see one, but the scars on the soul are difficult to see, unless you know what you are looking for.

It would seem that many men don't acknowledge what they are doing either, to them, this bending of the will, is acceptable. Here are two examples to illustrate the point.

This lady left her husband after 28 years, her words here are written as she spoke them.

"Looking back my husband controlled me right from the start, although it became gradually more and more over the years. Even when we decided to get married (no romantic proposal in sight) he said he would only marry me if I lost weight. I should have recognised the warning signals right then, but being young and in love with the prospect of getting married I agreed. Over the years any decisions I had to make were always joint decisions, and I had to run them by him before doing anything. That in itself made me personally very indecisive and insecure about doing anything before asking him. If I did make a decision on my own I always felt guilty.

He controlled me in all sorts of ways. He controlled the way I talked to people by always correcting me. Over many years this has made me insecure when talking to people, in case I say something wrong. He controlled my diet by always criticising my body shape and pinching my fat, and keeping watch over what I ate. Consequently I took to eating in secret to keep my eating habits to myself.

He controlled the fact that I wanted to smoke, but wouldn't let me, so I took to doing that in secret. He controlled the way we spent money and I always had to get approval for anything I wanted to buy. I ended up taking money out of the cashpoint rather than using my debit card so that he couldn't monitor my spending.

He wanted to monitor all my personal messages so I ended up having to lock my personal site on Facebook so that he couldn't access it.

He tended to take control of the way I spent my free time so that it suited him, and was not happy about me spending time with my own friends...he made me feel guilty in some way. For example, if I went out and came back late then he would always find some negative comment when I got back, or punish me by finding some task that he could have easily done, but saved it for me.

Worst of all was the way he wanted to control my visits abroad and even the way I spoke to my parents on the phone. He would monitor the length of my calls and look at me disapprovingly if he thought I was too long on the phone. I could never book flights abroad without his approval and then I would get an endless stream of negative comments, and usually have to pay for it when I returned home in some way.

With regard to trying to make me happy...there was very little he actually tried to do. Yes he did things around the house, and usually used those as some sort of reward. Flowers or other presents hardly ever happened...he's too mean for that. I wish that I had been stronger and never let him control me. I suppose in the beginning I didn't see it as control, but gradually over the years as I got wiser and realised that this was not normal behaviour I woke up to the fact that I could do the things I wanted to do without his approval.

My new life is beginning and it is strange to live everyday life without getting approval. It's going to take me a long time to get used to!

He took my independence away from me. I wasn't sure if I could cope with things on my own. It was not out of love for him that I stayed so long...just necessity! I feel so much more independent now. I didn't think I'd be able to cope on my own! How wrong I was.

I also dreaded the process of splitting up...having to tell the children and all our friends. It's been very hard. Sorting out all the money matters was also a difficult thing, but it's made me take control of my own finances which is a really good thing.

The thing is...there's no easy way to split up with someone, but if your life is as miserable as mine was...there is a way out. If you have the courage to go down that route then life will be better in the end.

After writing all this down and thinking back on things, God knows why I put up with it for so long!! He even used sex as a controlling device! I'm mad at myself for waiting so long to leave. However, the children are at the age now where they can understand my position better".

This second example, although shorter, is almost identical in the telling. This lady was another person in a very long term relationship and like the first lady, has since left her husband.

"Looking back he controlled me from day 1, I just didn't realise it. I was only 19 and he was 26. He decided what we did and where we went and what we spent money on (and how much). I was happy with this. I put down the deposit on the house and bought lots of the stuff for it. Again I was ok with this.

Problems started when I left work to have our daughter. I had no income and had to ask for even a fiver. He always wanted to know why I wanted money and I hated asking. This carried on for years. After my son was born I was very ill with post natal depression. I couldn't cope with his controlling the money and therefore me. One day when he got in from work I lost it and threw a mug at him. I got help and he opened his wallet. After that things were ok for a long time.

However, over the last few years it has gone downhill again. He wants to know where I am, who I am with, what time I will be home. Who am I texting/emailing? He tells me he loves me at least 6 times a day and says he would die without me. He buys me stuff all the time, lots of it expensive. It makes me feel like a cross between a trophy wife and a whore. But I, of course, accept it which does nothing for my self-esteem.

Sometimes I look in the mirror and I hate myself, other times I think life could be so much worse. I should have been much stronger right from the start. It's so easy to be wise with hindsight."

In only these two examples, and there were many more, time after time it comes across that the controlling began from the beginning. Guilt is used a lot, guilt over how they should be treated, or guilt over the children or how you made them look in front of people. Saving face is very important to the controlling male – the example that the lady said about correcting her language; in front of people, extremely belittling. Anything done on a daily basis has a cumulative effect and this is true of the mental cruelty that men put their wives through.

Interestingly all the questionnaires I received back on this matter were from married women and not co-habiters. Does this mean that the ring on the finger is another form of control that the name on a rental contract or mortgage doesn't have? Is this why the number of women leaving men is so much higher in proportion? If you remember it is 85% of women leave, compared to only 15% of men.

What then of the brave soul who decides it is time to leave? What method will the husband employ to keep her with him? One lady who took the survey had tried on a number of occasions to leave her husband but he kept pulling her back. On one occasion he put their son behind the car so that she couldn't back away. The latest occasion was all about the tears – he wailed on his hands and knees, begging her to stay. Not bad enough that he did it to her, but it was in front of the children. Her thought was that how could she leave him in those circumstances? How could she be seen by her children to be so cruel as to leave daddy crying? When she asked me this I pointed out that it was all about what he wanted, not what the children wanted, and definitely not what she wanted. His needs came before the family's and yet he made it appear that she would be the one breaking up the family.

A client from many years ago described how her husband would cry whenever she returned from work, after she had told him that she no longer loved him and was leaving.

If this book is about learning seduction, crying is not part of it. All women want a man in touch with his emotions, who can understand hers (as much as possible), but I don't know of any who like a man to cry to try and keep her.

How does a woman regain her sense of self after years of being belittled, had decisions about money and living taken away from her? How does a woman find who she really is? It seems that there is a point of clarity with all long term relationships, where the woman says enough is enough. It is also true that some women take a lot more convincing that their husband is an abuser than others. Many ladies feel that their partner doesn't abuse them because they are not hit, as in physically abused, but the emotional abuse is no less insidious or evil.

Universally your friends and family will tell you it is about time you came to your senses once you have left him; whilst you were with him people tolerated his ways because they love you. Once it's over then you will find what your friends and family really thought. If they had told you before, the decision would have been easier. Something happens and it is the straw that breaks the camel's back, the moment when she knows it is all over. In that moment a part of the person flows back; this is whether or not she has had an affair. It is the moment that she can no longer stay and once that idea forms so her plan to leave (or kick him out) begins. Once that decision is made you will also find that everything falls together very quickly.

As the lady said there is no easy way to split up with someone, but when it is over it is the only thing to do. When you walk out the door you must never look back, to look back or go back will mean more years of his control.

The promises of a better life, to take you on holiday, to do all the things you've always said you will do, all of this will fade after the initial burst of enthusiasm. The miser will become the giver, for a while, but his natural state will return as his habit falls back into place. Six months after you thought you were going to leave you will be looking out of your kitchen window wondering how it happened that you were still there whilst he is out fishing or at football and then you have to start the process all over again.

If you were going to do this with someone else has that person now moved on? If you had a house all set up who lives in it now? If you've told friends and family that you were going to leave him and you are still there how do they view you? In other words, now it is even harder and finding that courage becomes ever more difficult.

It is important to remember at this point that the person you are dealing with is a bully. He puts his needs before anyone else's and it isn't you that he cares about, it is his idea of who you should be. If you don't see yourself that way then it is time to leave.

In the Alfred Hitchcock film *Vertigo*, Scottie, the character played by James Stewart, turns the lady he meets into the exact image of his first wife. This is what he wants – the woman he sees you as, not the woman you are. This does rather beg the question – how do you see yourself?

The women who have helped with the research of this book have been predominantly in the 30-55 age group, broad I know, but if you've been with someone from the age of 17 then you know how much you've changed if you are 32, so imagine 42 or 52.

I have a friend who has known me since the age of 18; for a long time we didn't see each other, but in the last few years have grown closer as friends. I asked her how much I had changed since those early days and she told me I was unrecognisable from the young man she had known. Fortunately she meant in a positive way. If I have changed significantly then so will most of the people who have helped with the research (either as clients or contributors).

If your partner is still trying to get you to play a role then there is a high probability that you no longer feel comfortable playing that role and this is where the issues start. Like many things which have remained unchanged for a long time, it only needs a tiny crack for the whole structure to begin to fall apart. The Berlin Wall was a good example, rock solid for so many years and came down in a matter of days; a controlling relationship can fall apart just as quickly.

The key to understanding control is the chief weapon the husband uses. It is guilt and your susceptibility to it. If you have had an affair or you are in one as you read this you may have got past the subject of guilt in terms of cheating on your husband, but this is a private guilt, known only to you and your lover. The guilt that the husband uses is public guilt; by making you look a bad person, to blame you for the break-up of the marriage, to tell the children "I wanted to stay together, but Mummy broke us apart." Recognising this and seeing it for what it is is essential to breaking his hold over you.

Guilt is not a natural emotion like happiness or love or sadness; it is an emotion we are taught as small children. This is not remorse, to feel sorry for an act committed that hurts someone is good, but to suffer guilt is painful and pointless.

Who are you feeling guilty to? God? Your peers? Your children? It's all nonsense. Lose guilt and he loses his power. See things as they are, not worse than they are.

Shame is used in much the same way, the idea of shaming a person in public to make others think badly of her.

See the future: one month from now, six months from now, one year and five years from now. One day the pain will be behind you and although some of the after-shocks may be painful they will be nothing like the sorrow you will experience by staying as you are.

Re-read those words of the ladies with who changed their lives after 25+ years of suffering. You have one life and one life only, to look back with an ounce of regret when you could have changed your life will give you great sadness as you live out your days. Life is to be lived and lived with a passion and happiness that this sort of abuse sucks from you.

Domestic abuse is in all walks of life and needs to be recognised to raise its awareness. Physical abuse is more immediate and obvious, whereas many victims of psychological abuse accept their way of life as normal, when it isn't.

I'm yet to meet anyone who regrets walking away from a situation like this, that the 'married' life was better than being single when to be married was to be controlled.

By knowing that others have escaped from a situation like this only proves that it can be done, and it affects you, then I hope this section, in particular, has helped.

Key points to remember:

1   Domestic abuse is mentally controlling a person, rather than domestic violence which is by using physical pain to control a person. Both are as bad as each other.

2   Lady 1 – control came in many ways, from the amount of money she could spend to the sexual way she was controlled.

3   Lady 2 – money was a principle factor in this case, first of all limiting it and then thinking the answer was by trying to buy affection.

4   To understand that the abuser is a bully interested in only in his needs being met.

5   The principle weapon used against the victim is guilt. This is used in conjunction with shame.

6   There is a future, if you can find the belief and support, to search for it.

Chapter 16
The end is really the beginning

This book took me almost a year to write; hundreds of hours of research combined with years of personal experience and yet some of you will have read this in a day or less and if you've read every word then I praise you. So many people start a book and don't finish it; some books don't deserve to be finished and yet others deserve to be read more than once. There are around 70,000 plus words in this particular book, but there will be some that resonate more with you than others.

It was my desire to write a book that people would read, but I'd also like you to share it; perhaps you'll share the hard copy, but mostly I hope you will share the message and that message is that, as fundamentally different as we are as men and women, we all want to be loved. We express it very differently, but mostly we find a way to be connected.

As I have researched and written this piece I am aware of the changes in me. In my wild and crazy days I fully admit I did things which I am not particularly proud of, I feel regret for the people I hurt, but it's also true that there was fun along the way and on that journey I hope I brought some smiles. As we come to the end so we must go and practice what it preaches, but before we go I want to recap and add a story or two before I am tossed aside, to perhaps be reviewed again or until I see a copy in the window of a Help the Aged shop, then I'll know I have passed the full circle of literary life.

We began with the premise of how to seduce your wife, or for that matter anyone's wife; the proviso being, of course, that she had any interest in being seduced to begin with.

I have had men say to me, in the process of writing this, that I couldn't seduce their wife. A number of thoughts always came to me. One, if she is happy with you then you are absolutely correct. Two, who said I wanted to? My crazy days were behind me when I began writing this, although that's not to say that the research has not continued to be interesting. Three, the level of threat that men feel at the title of the book; I've heard of some men who want to punch me in the face – I'm sure this will increase if sales rise significantly – some men laugh out loud and don't know what to say. Others are intrigued.

The reaction from women has been almost universally positive; they find it unusual that a man wants to listen to them and to learn, although many have thought that getting the message across to men to be nigh on impossible. But I don't think so; men are funny creatures, some keep their feelings to themselves, others wear them like a badge of honour. Others cry at the slightest provocation, some never cry at anything at all. What we all share is the desire to be loved; I have a friend who is one of the toughest men I've ever met. He has served in the armed forces on active duty, has been shot at many times and when he came out of the Army worked on the doors for ten years and yet to see him with the woman he loves you'd think he was the softest, sweetest guy you'd ever met. To a degree you'd be correct as well, he is, but he has that yin-yang balance of extreme toughness mixed with a heart of marshmallow. If you saw him with his grandchildren you'd be even more struck by the love he shows for them and his sense of family.

Human beings are pretty simple creatures, we have the basic needs as laid out by Abraham Maslow: food and shelter, a sense of purpose, love and intimacy, levels of self-esteem and the final philosophical point, to know your place in the world.

When this book is released I will have been on a journey for almost 8 years, from my first unsteady steps away from what I knew (monogamy and many years with the same person) to a rich and varied adventure. Along the way there have been relationships, there has been insane and all-consuming love, there has been heart break and pain as well as ecstasy and sexual experimentation that I could never have believed would happen to me.

Every step of the way has been about learning, about myself, about people I have spent time with, about clients I have helped and friends and supporters whom I have shared these tales with. I sat down to write this book because I know there are people who need help and don't have the time or inclination to tread the path I have been on. Nor should they either.

I come at this subject from a very different perspective to the greats like Allan and Barbara Pease, John Grey and Alfred Kinsey. All of them were in settled relationships when they did their research and wrote their books. I have spent much of the time on this journey as a single man, walking the path of dating sites, random meetings, third hand conversations and first hand experiences.

If you are coming out of a long term relationship in 2015 (or whenever you read this) then it is confusing and, at times, bloody scary. My hope is that by reading this it has helped you avoid the minefields and keep you on the path to love and security.

If you are in a relationship and you want to keep your partner then I hope these things you have read here helped you stay together and if you are single I hope that it has opened your eyes to the massive possibilities of love and sex in this century of information overload. Some of you may have wished that I had further researched the worlds of Grindr, Tinder and Adult Friend Finder. I am grateful to those who shared their knowledge with me so that I didn't have to research those any deeper than I did. It became quite evident as I wrote these words that common themes kept occurring and the most obvious one was the lack of romance in the world and how intrusive social media has become in our day to day communication. Smart phones are making us dumb. Even those of us who complain still spend far too much time on them and usually only to check Facebook or to read another spam email. We have become expert at dealing with things that are shallow instead of spending more time on those things which affect us with depth.

When I was a child I could lose myself in a game of soldiers, drawing or watching *Thunderbirds* or the adventures of Simon Templar. Our television had three channels, all of them were in black and white and even then it was enough. Now we have every audio and visual stimulus you could possibly imagine and technology drives us further from our real purpose. To communicate and procreate.

I wonder how I would have grown up had my parents stayed together and if my mother hadn't sat talking to me all that time. I wonder what I gave her? It is probably because I had so little idea what she was saying that I learned how to listen and that skill has been one of the most important I've ever learnt. I did ask her what she used to tell me, she said "Same old rubbish I tell you now!" She laughed and thought it was hilarious.

So many people don't seem to have these listening skills and are distracted by all that is going on around them, which is bad news for relationships and for our default settings. We know that in the early days we are fully engaged and want to know everything about our new partner; we know that by doing this the love will grow (or the like) and the sex will be better. We are in the moment with each other, but often it fades so quickly and that's when the problems start. That taking each other for granted and then one (or both parts of the couple) responding to Jimmy Mack (remember him?) and the next thing you know another relationship comes to a crashing end, more pain, more tears and time to start all over again.

It is a fine line we walk, to be with someone who makes us feel good and to not accept anyone who makes us feel less than a princess or a prince. Relationship is about building on the human experience. Tony Robbins talks about this.

Imagine going to see your favourite band and there are only 10 of you there, of course you'd get more time with them, but you wouldn't get that buzz of seeing them with 600 people and definitely not the connection you get in an arena of 10,000 people. Relationship enhances the human experience. True love deepens that experience, when you find someone who 'gets you'. So why would we ever let that pass? And yet we do; I talked earlier about neglect and this is what we must strive to avoid, at all costs. Do you want to seduce your wife? Then be connected with her, not in a stalker way, but in a way that makes her know you care. If you don't you run the risk of her head being turned by someone else. We never know when someone fancies us and each day we don't know who we might meet.

Every day has the potential for you to find your ideal partner; this is as true for couples as it is for singles.

Like all things worth having, a great relationship requires continuous work and continuous attention. I also recognise that sometimes it's difficult. If you run your own business that will take your time, if you have children they will take your time, then there is your social life, your hobbies and any other interests you may have which compete for you time, but no matter what if you want to keep the person you love you'd better make them know that they are loved. This means their strategy for love, not yours.

Cast your mind back to the points scoring method a woman has, cutting the grass is not a high scoring love strategy; telling her she's beautiful is. Even this can be fraught with danger though and as you get older you realise this, if you've upset her in some way telling her she looks beautiful can make her think you're trying to get round her. No one ever said this was going to be simple. It is worth the effort though, if you've found the right one. But what if you haven't? What if you realise that the packaging on the box, doesn't match the contents inside? This is when you have to act quickly, for both your sakes. A long, miserable relationship is much worse than no relationship at all.

Seduction also comes from within. One of the exercises I get clients to do is to imagine their ideal partner; I do this for both sexes, but for now let's imagine we are talking to a female.

She is in her early 50's and is looking for someone new, she has been in a relationship for nearly 20 years and the thought of looking for love and companionship scares the life out of her, so to help her I get her to describe her ideal man.

He's 5' 6" to 6'4", white, blue-grey eyes, dark to greying hair, in good shape, but not obsessed with exercise. He's intelligent and has his own money, whether that's a business or a good job. He dresses well, he is funny, he likes to try new things and, of course, he is great in bed. This is her shopping list for her ideal man and then I ask her this question.

"Do you believe that you could attract a man who looked and acted like that?"

All of a sudden doubt absorbs her and she thinks she is asking for too much. If he is this ideal man is she good enough to be his ideal woman? Of course the answer is yes, but when your confidence is low, when you've been neglected for a long time and you don't realise you are attractive it all comes as a bit of shock to be told you are. To become beautiful and desired is an inside and an outside job. There is much to be done in this journey of love and seduction and most of it is on ourselves. There are a number of questions that you should ask yourself on a regular basis:

"What does this mean to me?"

"Who is making my life less than wonderful?"

"Who will I meet today?"

"What will I have fun with today?"

"What will I learn today?"

Each one of these questions can be asked at any time throughout the day and all are designed to help you grow and to develop. A person who grows is one who is interesting to others, those conversations that only involve the children, work or money are going to sap your energy and see your partner as a partner in the business of being an adult. Most of us would admit that is totally over-rated.

Look at your children or remember when they were small. Weren't they fun? Didn't you love to watch them play, to draw, to make their own music? Ok, maybe you wanted to lock them in their room then, but it was their sense of play that was so infectious. Remember how much fun your partner was, think of what sort of partner you want to attract. Unless you like dour, unless you want a serious person isn't what we really want is a partner in the game of life? Someone who understands it is a game and not the person who escapes life at the bottom of a glass, a toke of a joint, or in the mindless affairs of the lonely or disconnected.

If you came to this book looking for ways to seduce someone else's wife then you might have found some new methods of doing it, but I also doubt that that person got this far in the book. This book is about commitment, but it is also to remind people that life is short and should be lived to the full. We hear it all the time and yet we still take time for granted.

Have you ever had a lot of money and somehow found that soon enough it all disappeared? The thing with money is that there is always a way to make more; time isn't like that. Once it's gone, it's gone. You never get to live today again, is that why time travel appeals to us so much? A bit like *Groundhog Day*, we want to do some days over and over until we get it right. Equally there are some days which you wish would end almost as soon as they started. If time is such a precious commodity why do we waste so much of it? I'm not saying duvet days are not to be savoured, they are, so is laying on a beach and doing nothing, but not for too long and equally not with the person who drags you down.

There have been so many occasions that I have heard people say "Why did I spend so much time on that person? I feel like I've wasted my life." Who can answer that? Should you have left earlier? Possibly, but regret doesn't get you very far.

One of the reasons I went into so much detail on the six options you have when you think a relationship is finished is that I want you to be sure. And to make it clear, you absolutely don't have to go through all six options obviously, sometimes there is only one. Leave and leave now.

A friend of mine, during the writing process, told me it took her four years to leave her husband, from when she initially thought about it. That was one of the longest relationships that came to an end, over thirty years. She also said that every seven years there was a new crisis and when it came around the fourth time that was when she finally lost patience – and it still took four years to leave.

My longest relationship that I knew lasted too long was three-and-a-half years and back then I was not the more decisive person I am now. I had two affairs in that time and finally walked away when I knew it was over. This was incredibly stupid of me; I should have walked when I first had an affair. You know why I didn't? Fear. That same old reason for why we don't make decisions, we are so bloody scared of getting it wrong and yet, the irony is, that by staying where we are when we are not happy we are lying to ourselves and our partner. We have to learn to see the future. What do we want to happen? Where do we want to go? What dream do we want to pursue?

When I was in my longest relationship my focus was entirely on building my martial arts school and learning martial arts; when I got into psychology I then started to dilute my interest in martial arts as I strove to build a client base in the therapy business. Can you guess what happened? I did both things really badly and in the process harmed my relationship. My focus was all over the place.

As a young boy I wanted to be a writer and wrote five novels, westerns, from the age of 13 to 14. All long hand and all long gone. It never occurred to me write another book for many years. I'd write articles for martial arts magazines and I even once had a piece in the *Daily Mail*, but my desire to be a writer never left me. The only difference was a complete lack of dedication.

Near the end of my relationship Hayley and I were talking and she asked what I wanted to do. I told her. "I want to write, I want to express my thoughts and I want people to be interested enough to buy my books. I want to go into Waterstones and see my book on the shelves." We parted about a year after that and it would still be six years before I wrote my first book "The Magic Number" which came out in November 2013.

Why did it take me so long when all I had ever professed to do was write?

Fear.

The exact same emotion that you feel when you can't decide if you are going to leave your partner. The exact emotion you feel when you want to ask that girl (or boy) out. The same emotion you have when your mind gets in the way of your ambitions. If we were all psychic we'd make decisions so much more easily; we'd know what the outcome was going to be, but instead we become paralysed with what we already know.

The first of the six human needs is certainty. With the person we have now (no matter how ill suited, how boring, how abusive) that person knows us and in our minds that is better than having no one at all or someone else who might be worse. What a horrific way of living your life. To have such a dim view of your future, to settle for such a poor quality of life, you owe it to yourself, and your children, if you have any, to live a life that is exciting, rewarding and fulfilling.

Do you remember my rascal of a friend Tony, the three in a night and £25 profit guy? He was one of my closest friends and when he died part of me went with him. Who would I talk to about these crazy thoughts? Whose advice could I ask? The answer came when I was at my most lonely and when I was acting in my most debauched way, the answer was inside me and so it is with you. If you want a better quality of relationship then demand it first of yourself and then of your partner, whether you are with them now or for whom you allow into your life. You know what sort of person you want; you know who would make you happy, so why would you settle for anything less?

In the process of writing this book I have become more aware that my idea of love is different to many people; as if I expect more because I want to give more. Great sex is important to me because I think it fuels the passion and the passion fuels the sex, but it is the overall feeling of all consuming, beautiful, rewarding, honest love that is so important to me.

I lied a lot in my wild days, so much so that sometimes I struggled to tell the truth, but now I am honest, almost transparent and I expect that of my partner too. Without trust, without honesty we only live a lie. That's part of the message of this book, be true to yourself. Know what you want, people will treat you the way you allow them to. When I looked at the domestic abuse situation this became totally clear; that erosion of self-belief and all done with a smile and kind word. From the outside it was hard for people to see the true state of the relationship.

How often do we look at other people and think they have everything sorted? The perfect couple, the successful businessman, the rock star, the together guy.

In 2014 Robin Williams committed suicide, who saw that coming? It was a total shock, he had everything going for him; we subsequently learned that he had early symptoms of Parkinson's Disease as well as struggling with depression. My point here is that none us of know anyone else's daily battles, so if we are struggling it would be fair to assume that some of our family and friends are as well. We are not alone in the game of life, a much nicer phrase than the daily struggle, don't you think?

It's ok to ask for help and it's ok to accept that your relationship might just be awful. You're not the only one.

It may have been that as you read this through this book that you were looking for the defining moment of how you seduce your wife, anyone else's or for that matter your business partner's or your work mate's. If you have thought that seduction is all about sex then you have not got the message across. Seduction is just another word for connection but if I called this book "How to connect with your wife or anyone else's" would you have ever bought it? I doubt it. Don't feel cheated, the answer is still the same whichever semantics you use.

You have to find out what turns your partner on (sexually and otherwise) and do more and more of it.

One of the ladies in the sex survey is a submissive, she wants her man to tell her exactly what to do and she will do it for him, sexually or otherwise. She gives herself to him completely, if you go back over the sex survey she was one of the ladies who was beaten, and she found it turned her on. For many people this is not the lifestyle they would choose to live, but it is done with respect and with honesty and no matter what your thoughts are on the matter it works for them.

Near the end of writing of the book she confessed to me that their relationship was now almost completely vanilla i.e.as it is with many other couples, but what works for other couples wasn't what she wants from the relationship. As she put it "He hasn't beaten me for months." It sounds strange, but it was what she wanted.

If you've read *50 Shades of Grey* you'll know that this is what all the controversy was about, the beatings, the whipping, the violation of Anastasia. Some people were up in arms about this, ironically most of the kink community because of the way that E.L. James had portrayed Christian Grey as a 'damaged' individual. The kink community totally refuted the idea that to become a 'dom' or a 'sub' you must have been abused as a child.

What made the lady's relationship work was not only the normal vanilla lifestyle, but also the rough or dominating sex. Without it felt that the spark had gone; at the time of writing they had been together for three years and many relationship experts will tell you that you can't keep the spark going indefinitely, but I disagree. You can, but you have to focus on your relationship and make it a priority, you have to keep your eye on the prize, the prize being love.

I have a friend who is an advanced driving instructor and we were talking about car crashes and why they happen. Too often speed is blamed for accidents; I've also discussed this with an air ambulance doctor and he agreed with the following theory.

Speed is not why a lot of people have accidents or die in them. The reason so many accidents happen is that the driver stops concentrating on driving; he/she is doing something else other than driving the car. We know how many distractions there can be: changing the station on the radio, looking at your phone, talking on the phone, putting a cd in, doing your make up or just day dreaming. When we first learned to drive it seemed so complex; how to change gear whilst keeping your eyes on the road, judging braking distances, clutch control, knowing when to change gear by the sound of the engine and/or the rev counter, your head spins and everything seems to go so fast. Relatively speaking though it wasn't long before it all seemed second nature, easy and when you're driving along the motorway at 60mph why do you have to concentrate fully? That's literally what we think, we're bored. It's funny how 60mph doesn't seem so slow when you're trying to brake in a hurry.

It's the same process with a relationship. We start by giving everything, all of our attention, when the person comes to our house we're showered, shaved, we smell good. Six months down the line we have a quick wash of the armpits and genitals and a spray of something nice and smelly and we're good to go. A year down the line and we're probably living with each other and having farting competitions on the sofa watching the Great British Bake Off. Three years down the line and we're coming home late, seeing each other as you pass in the hallway on the way to work and after ten years all we do is complain at how they don't let us watch what we want to watch on TV or we can't get a sensible word out of them.

If the number one human need is certainty then when we have it in bucket loads, we're bored. We're bored of life, of love, of our partner and of our life. And here comes Jimmy Mack and Alfie Elkins and Beryl most certainly is interested. Who can blame her? You've stopped caring, you've stopped trying and you've stopped concentrating. To revisit our analogy the car crash is about to happen.

If you are now rolling your eyes and thinking "Oh my God, does this mean I have to try harder?" then congratulations. You've got it right. You have to try a lot harder and hope to Christ that you haven't left it too late.

I've known of plenty of times when that has happened. The wife in this case is thinking "Why didn't he do this three years ago?" When you've fallen out of love with someone nothing is more annoying than your partner doing their very best to impress you. It's like trying to bring life back to a neglected shoe, no matter how much you polish it that thing is still going to look dull and tarnished.

I have heard of many cases where a man tried to gain his woman back by giving her ultimatums or by changing things in the house or by throwing money at the issues, as if jewellery or a new car is going to make the difference. Why do we fall in love? Because the person we fall in love with is making us feel like there has never been anyone else and nor will there be. They think of our needs, our desires, what will make us happy. When the relationship is bad it is all about what they want, how you don't make them feel happy. As the New Radicals said "You get what you give" – and we are talking emotion, not in manipulative gifts.

As we wind our way towards the final pages I'll bring together the essence of what this book is all about, the answer to the question of how to seduce anyone be they wife, husband, any form of sexual partner, business associate , friend or new customer. It comes down to a couple of things, giving the feeling first being one of them. Another is communication, what you talk about and how you listen. That word seduce conjures up all sorts of expectations. In the *Dead Poets Society* John Keating (played by Robin Williams) say "Words and ideas can change the world," and that "Language was invented for the art of wooing women." If that is true, and I believe both statements are, then why are people so bad at it?

For all the reasons we have already discussed: not listening, head being somewhere else, losing the passion etc, etc so here we are at the crux.

How to become the master seducer?

If I was writing about this in a business sense I would be talking more about body language, the way you dress, the feelings you express and the cultural beliefs that would work best for you and all of that would be true in order to establish rapport and a successful business relationship. However, this book is about love and so it is that I will request your indulgence at these final ideas.

Those of you with good memories may remember some of the next section as I opened chapter one with the following words. I wanted you to know from the off that this wasn't a book for picking up women. I wrote it to help people find a deeper place for their soul and the love affair they were in or they wanted. As you revisit them take me with you all the way to end where the final words will give you the answer you seek.

For me to be in love is about three distinct areas: physical, emotional and spiritual. The physical is always the easiest to understand. If you are intensely attracted to someone then the emotions are affected anyway, obviously you get turned on, but you will also find your heart leap, your life feels better immediately and there is sunshine everywhere you look.

A smile, a kiss, a gentle touch, all elicit emotions of passion and happiness, serotonin and oxytocin is released and you float off into the world of love. Can you have great sex without love? Yes, you can. Can you have love without great sex? I'd argue it's more difficult.

I understand that you can be in love with someone and do a lot of things that don't involve sex, but great, passionate, heart stopping sex fuels your passion even further. To wrap someone up in your arms is to feel a closeness that you can't get from anywhere else. Most of my writing of the last few years has been fuelled by the passions that women have stirred up in me. My understanding of loneliness, my coping mechanisms, my desire to give every part of myself has been driven by someone whom I loved. It started with a kiss and it was driven by crazy, wonderful sex, but that wasn't all.

The gentle touch of a hand in a darkened cinema, walking in the countryside and holding hands, just to look at the one you love sitting on a rock by a gurgling stream, all of this is the physical manifestations which have affected me so deeply at an emotional level.

The emotion of love is so all consuming it is true that you do actually go mad, that to think of that person who fills your heart with joy can stop all thoughts in your tracks. To feel love so deeply that you forget to breathe and only become aware of it when you have to take the next breath. To hold someone in your arms on a chill morning and smell their hair as they snuggle tighter into your chest. How can emotions not be intrinsically linked?

Finally to the spiritual. That feeling beyond emotion, beyond the most intense orgasm, beyond even the thrill of looking at each other in the moment your eyes lock together, when you go beyond what you think is physically and emotionally possible and reach a high you have never reached before.

To give yourself so deeply to someone that you are convinced they will never be interested in another person again. To give all of this and to be touched like a person catching the most beautiful sunset, the sound of your baby's first cry or your mother's "I love you", to feel all of this is to transcend all previous love. To know that no matter what, you must be with this person for the rest of your life, as long as the love flows and you keep being connected.

In the introduction I told you I am a romantic and I described my version of romance, what is different now, as I have realised in the writing – and hopefully you have in the reading – is that romance is so much more than what we have been taught to expect.

Romance is the giving of the soul. It is not superficial presents or the act of calculation, it is the supreme act of giving. It is the giving of your soul and it also the receiving of everything that the person you love wants to give you. All of their dreams, all of their desire, all of their passion.

It is also about taking their hand and helping them through their fears and together, as in the best fairytales, you walk hand in hand towards the sunset where your future lies and the best of you resides.

That is how you seduce your wife and if you do that there will never be anyone else's to think about.

Key points to remember:

1   **It's ok to show your emotions, but don't lose control**
2   **We exist to communicate and procreate**

3   Seduction comes from within
4   Asking powerful questions
5   Overcoming your fears
6   We don't know other people's struggles
7   A relationship is like learning to drive
8   The relationship triad: physical, emotional and spiritual
9   How you seduce your wife

Bibliography

Brendon, M (2008). *Swinging - The Games Your Neighbours Play*. London: The Friday Project. p170-p182

Gathorne-Hardy, J. (2005). *Kinsey, A Biography*. London: Pimlico. p395

Gray, J. (1992). *Men Are From Mars, Women Are From Venus*. London: Harper Collins Publishers.

James, E.L. (2012). *50 Shades of Grey*. London: Random House

Kinsey, A.C., Pomeroy, W.B & Martin, C.E. (1948). *Sexual Behaviour in the Human Male*. Philadelphia: Saunders.

Kinsey, A.C., Pomeroy, W.B & Martin, C.E. (1953). *Sexual Behaviour in the Human Female*. Philadelphia: Saunders.

Lister, A. (2006). *Swingers True Confessions From Today's Swinging Scene*. London: Random House. p63-p132

Strauss, N. (2005). *The Game*. Edinburgh: Cannongate Books.

Filmography

Alfie (1966) Film, Directed by: Gilbert, L., USA: Paramount

Any Given Sunday (1999) Film, Directed by: Stone, O., USA: Warner Bros.

Bram Stoker's Dracula (1992) Film, Directed by: Coppola, F.F., USA: American Zoetrope & Osiris Films

Brief Encounter (1945) Film, Directed by: Lean, D., USA: Eagle Lion Distributors

Brokeback Mountain (2005) Film, Directed by: Lee, A., USA: Focus Features

Connolly, B (2007) *On Religion* on *Was It Something I Said?* (DVD) London, Universal Pictures

Don Juan De Marco (1994) Film, Directed by: Leven, J., USA: New Line Cinema

Gone With The Wind (1939) Film, Directed by: Fleming, V., USA: Metro-Goldwyn-Mayer

Jerry Maguire (1996) Film, Directed by: Crowe, C., USA: Tristar Pictures

Life Is Beautiful (1998) Film, Directed by: Begnini, R., USA: Miramax Films

Love Actually (2003) Film, Directed by: Curtis, R., UK: Working Title Films

Notting Hill (1999) Film, Directed by: Mitchell, R., UK: Working Title Films

The Notebook (2004) Film, Directed by: Cassavetes, N., USA: New Line Cinema

The Princess Bride (1987) Film, Directed by: Reiner, R., USA: 20th Century Fox

Discography.

Diamond, N., Bergman, A., & Bergman, M (1978) *You Don't Bring Me Flowers* on *I'm Glad You're Here With Me Tonight* (Album) New York, Columbia Records

Grohl, D., (1997) *Everlong* on *The Colour and The Shape* (Album) Seattle, Roswell Records

Holland, B., Dozier, L., & Holland, E., (1967) *Jimmy Mack* (Single) Detroit. Motown.

Morrison, J., & White, E.G., (2006) *You Give Me Something* on *Undiscovered* (Album) London, Universal

About the author:

How to seduce your wife (or anyone else's) is Andy Gibney's second book. His first, *The Magic Number*, was published in November 2013. Since 2002 he has been a therapist, first of all specialising in curing phobias, but in time helped more and more people with relationship issues related to depression and more commonly, anxiety. As time passed he could see the trends that formed which led him to further research.

His personal life went through a number of changes after a long term relationship ended in 2007 and the lessons he learned on the way are also included in the book. He has performed hundreds of talks as an inspirational speaker and still teaches martial arts at his centre in Northamptonshire. He also lives in the county.